Praise for Bass for B

Perfect for beginners looking to be self taught

"I am about half-way through this book and I've gone from knowing nothing about the bass to already playing measures to songs. No one is going to be made into expert for reading and following, but I have been impressed with how far I've come. It definitely gives a good foundation. I already bought the bass fret book; which I plan to devour after I have finished working my way through this book."

—Scott In Milwaukee

Great overview of the bass!

"This book is a fantastic overview of what a bass player needs to know. It will not, however, replace the work needed to apply that knowledge to your instrument. You still have to practice 'till you love it and then play 'till you're annoying someone. My favorite aspect of the transaction: The backing and sample tracks are a snap to download - they are mp3's that come all in one shot in a ZIP, so if you have a little storage room they are yours for life. The book is well written and a pretty entertaining read. It is one of the few bass books I've acquired that will gather dog-ear pages instead of dust. I like it!"

— *Avg Joe*

Fun to read

"Yes, it can get detailed at times. But, it does not throw you into the deep end right away. Easy lessons in each chapter. Well written. Basics and foundation techniques here. Giving you a rock solid start. Highly recommend it. It's not just a once read. I will be practicing the lessons for the next few weeks."

—D C McKay

BASS

FOR

BEGINNERS

How to Play the Bass Guitar in
7 Simple Steps Even if You've
Never Picked up a Bass Before

 **GUITAR HEAD**

GH@theguitarhead.com
www.facebook.com/theguitarhead/

Disclaimer

Please note the information contained within this document is for educational and entertainment purposes only. Every attempt has been made to provide accurate, up to date and reliable complete information. No warranties of any kind are expressed or implied. Readers acknowledge that the author is not engaging in the rendering of legal and financial, medical or professional advice. The content of this book has been derived from various sources. Please consult a licensed professional before attempting any techniques outline in this book.

By reading this document, the reader agrees that under no circumstances are is the author responsible for any losses, direct or indirect, which are incurred as a result of the use of information contained within this document, including, but not limited to, — errors, omissions, or inaccuracies.

Dedication

We dedicate this book to the complete
Guitar Head team,
supporters, well-wishers and
the Guitar Head community.

It goes without saying that we
would not have gotten
this far without
your encouragement,
critique and support.

Contents

Free Guitar Head Bonuses

Audio Files

All Guitar Head books come with audio tracks for the licks inside the book. These audio tracks are an integral part of the book - they ensure you are playing the charts and chords the way they are intended to be played.

Lifetime access to Guitar Head Community

Being around like-minded people is the first step to being successful at anything. The Guitar Head community is a place where you can find people who are willing to listen to your music, answer your questions or talk anything music.

Email newsletters sent directly to your inbox

We send regular musical lessons and tips to all our subscribers. Our subscribers are also the first to know about Guitar Head giveaways and holiday discounts.

Free PDF

We wrote a book about 25 of the most common mistakes guitarists make and decided to give it for free to all Guitar Head readers.

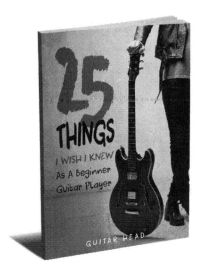

You can grab a copy of the free book, audio files and subscribe to newsletter by following the link below.

All these bonuses are a 100% free, with no strings attached. You won't need to enter any personal details other than your first name and email address.

To get your bonuses, go to: ***www.theguitarhead.com/bonus***

Introduction

So you like the bass guitar, huh?

Maybe it was the lightning-fast fingers of Les Claypool that first inspired you. Perhaps it was the punk rock energy of Flea that put the fire in you. Was it the smooth, inventive jazz of Charles Mingus? Heck, it could even be the subdued yet essential basslines of The Beatles thanks to Sir Paul McCartney.

The forefront of popular music is often dominated by the lead vocalists and guitarists of a band. With big sounds—and even bigger personalities—their musical contributions tend to take center stage in the public eye. Yet you and I both know that even the greatest melodies ever written would end up sounding hollow, weak, and unremarkable without the foundational bedrock of a bass guitar in the mix.

Nothing gets the heart pumping or the feet moving quite like the sound of a bass guitar—so kudos to you for taking an interest in this 4-stringed beast! The world is a better place with your groovy beats in it. Now go and share those gifts with your legion of fans!

... What's that?

You don't know how to play bass yet?

You mean you've never even held a bass before?

Perfect!

Like any instrument, the bass guitar contains many intricacies that could take years of practice to fully understand and unlock.

However, the bass is also remarkably simple to grasp its fundamentals—and a fledgling musician of any skill level can start plucking notes and following rhythms in no time!

I get it. You're skeptical. You're worried your lack of experience is too much of a hurdle to climb over. No doubt there are dozens of concerns racing through your mind like:

- ✔ I don't even know what a bass is!

- ✔ How am I supposed to hold a bass??

- ✔ I don't know what to do with my left hand!

- ✔ I don't know what to do with my right hand!

- ✔ Reading music scares me.

- ✔ Rhythm and tempo scare me.

- ✔ Marilyn Manson scares me. (I can't help you with this one.)

Don't sweat. We're gonna take this nice and easy through 7 Simple Steps that have been carefully designed to bring you up to speed, starting with the very core fundamentals all the way to playing your first 12-bar blues.

Even if you have no understanding of musical notation, or you've never played an instrument before, I promise that by the end of this book you will surprise even yourself with how well you can pick through some funk-tastic basslines!

That's it. 7 steps. So are you ready to get started?

Let's go!!

Explaining the Bass Guitar

"Say hello to my little friend!"

OK, so it's not that little.
But it's definitely a potential friend for life.

Let's learn more about what the Bass Guitar is, what
it's for, how it's put together, and how you should
hold this magnificent musical instrument.

CHAPTER 1

Basic Principles of the Bass Guitar

The stronger that the bass can support all the other instruments, the more the other guys can shine... something I like to stress in being a bass player is the spirit of givingness."

– Flea

What's up with the bass, and why would anyone want to play it?

Mr. Michael Balzary, AKA Flea, phrased it much better than I could ever dream of doing. In that quote, which he stated in an hour-long bass lesson promoting his own brand of basses (Flea Bass), he touched upon the essential principles of the bass guitar, and ultimately of being a bass player.

One of these principles is that the bass is often considered to be the foundation, both harmonically and rhythmically, of music.

He also describes the instrument as a wonderful accompaniment and form of support for a band.

Oh, and he also hints why all this doesn't necessarily have to be true 100% of the time.

Before we get into the technicalities of playing bass guitar, let's take a look at each of those points, as it's important to know *why* the instrument you're hoping to learn even exists in the first place.

The Base of Bass

First of all, what exactly is "bass"? In audio terms, the word *bass* refers to anything that's producing the lower frequencies and/or notes of a particular piece of music or soundscape. Many instruments other than the bass guitar serve this function in different styles of music, such as the double bass in classical, the tuba in marching bands, or mono synthesizers in electronic music.

The bass part executed by these instruments combines with the bass notes of other instruments (such as the bass drum) to form the low end of the music. This "low end" might be somewhat inaudible to the untrained ear, but it can certainly be felt (it's what makes the floor vibrate or creates those thumps and booms from certain cars in traffic).

The "natural" function of this low spectrum in the music is to be a foundation, a base, the bedrock upon which the rest of the music is erected and brought to life. When we study harmony, you'll notice that the root note played by the bass instruments usually dictates the whole tonality of the piece, and therefore the chords that can or can't be played (depending on whether you're into dissonance or not) at a certain moment.

The Role of The Bass Player

In modern music, the bass player in any sort of ensemble holds both the harmonic base and rhythmic base on his or her shoulders.

The bassist isn't alone of course; percussion and drums are essential to a rhythm section, and so are the rest of the more melodic instruments—but it's important when starting out to know where the bass usually stands in music, so that playing with other people comes naturally at first.

In a usual jazz, rock, or blues ensemble (a band with a drummer,guitarists, pianists, singers...), the bass player and the drummer form the rhythm section. So the bassist must keep one eye on the drummer, particularly on the bass drum, and another eye on the melodic players.

Now, that doesn't have to be completely true 100% of the time. It's very normal for bassists, or any musician really, to drift off and hog the ball when they feel that it's their moment to shine... and this is OK! But it should be never be done to the detriment of the song and the overall sound of the band. Everyone is a team player!

That being said, there are many bass players that have broken these "rules" completely and achieved groundbreaking results with their bass guitar.

For example, Les Claypool from Primus writes most of his music on a bass, so his bass lines usually carry the melodic themes in his music. There's also Evan Brewer and Jaco Pastorius, who apart from playing in well-known ensembles as true team players, have also released "bass only" albums where the bass is the soloing instrument.

These exceptions to the rule should inspire you, but don't let them dissuade you from fulfilling the classic role of the bass player with other musicians. Music is at its best when everyone comes together and harmoniously adds to the whole. Then again, there's no rule that says that you have to do one or the other—so above all, express yourself and have fun!

In the end, this slab of wood with 4 strings is nothing but a tool. It's your choice to use it however you want and to become whoever you want. If you follow your true nature and maintain that spirit of givingness, then the music is gonna shine!

CHAPTER II

The Bass Guitar and Its Parts

No matter what you prefer playing, you should get to know your instrument on both a unique and a general level.

With "general" I mean the parts that make up the instrument, regardless of whether it's the bass guitar that guy in that band you like uses — or *your* personal bass guitar.

"Unique," as you probably imagined, means the little nuances that only your instrument has. Both are quite important in your journey as a bass guitarist, so let us now look at the parts that make up a bass.

First, we have the **body** (**#1**) which is just a big ole slab of wood. The body helps with the overall resonance of the instrument, even if most of the work making sound is done by the **pickups** (**#2**). The body and the wood it's made from matter a great deal, because the vibrations produced by the pickups have to come from somewhere.

The pickups, which are always placed on the body and under the strings, are basically microphones that are specially designed to capture the vibrations of the strings. The strings become amplified by the acoustics of the body, which then turns these vibrations into the electric signals that go to an amplifier.

To do that, you got a bunch of electronics underneath the pickups that go into the output **jack** (**#3**), which is the part you connect to the amp. Depending on where the output jack is located on your particular bass (usually on top of the body or on the lower side), you should consider purchasing either a straight cable or an "L-shaped" or "angled" cable.

Moving away from the body, we have the **neck** (**#4**). This solid piece of wood is designed to hold the **fretboard** (**#5**), which is a thinner piece of flat wood that's glued to the neck and holds the **frets** (**#6**), which are those little pieces of metal that separate the board into the spaces where your fingers go, with each space corresponding to an exact note. There are of course also fretless basses, but they're a bit more challenging for players just starting out.

At the top of the neck we have the **headstock** (**#7**), which almost always belongs to the same piece of wood. The headstock is equipped with those little mechanisms called **tuning pegs** (**#8**). These are there to tighten the strings and regulate their tension (also known as tuning), along with the **bridge** (**#9**), which is that little piece of metal at the bottom of the body.

And since we're back on the body, what are those **knobs (#10)** over by the output jack? Though their functions can vary a lot from bass to bass, they are usually a **volume** knob and some sort of **tone** control. "Tone" here refers to the different frequencies you feed the amp from the ones resonating throughout the body. That's right, the sound varies depending on what part of the bass is vibrating. Try the following exercise:

Without an amp, grab your bass and a pick and play really close to where the neck starts, but still on the body. What do you perceive from that sound? Is it more warm and rich in low frequencies? Now try playing right next to the bridge. How does that sound? Is it a lot brighter and more intense on the mid-frequencies?

That variation in sound is the reason why most electronic stringed instruments have several pickups. In the bass on the diagram (which is a Fender Jazz Bass), we've got a **neck pickup** and a **bridge pickup**. The tone control on the knobs lets you settle on a mix between the sound of both pickups, or just have them all turned up all the way to enjoy the full sonic scale of the instrument.

Lastly, some basses have a piece of plastic that surrounds the pickups. This is called a **pickguard (#11)**, and it's there in part to protect the precious wood from being damaged by your pick (if you use one).Through the years, however, it's mostly been left there merely for aesthetic purposes.

What's Unique About My Instrument?

To close this chapter off, I'd like to encourage you to play close attention to the instrument you've chosen to learn. Bear in mind that it's made out of wood, which used to be a living thing—and no two living things are identical on this earth.

As much as it was probably made in a factory by automated processes, instruments still feature some degree of human labor in their production, and even the work of machines suffers from variation.

Also, consider that the circumstances surrounding your instrument and how it made its way to you are quite unique as well. Maybe it was owned and loved by an enthusiast for decades. Maybe it never left someone's attic until it was sold to you. Perhaps the wood of your instrument came from a tall, majestic mahogany tree somewhere in Peru.

All of these things alter the feel and affect the sound of your instrument. The height of the strings, the type of strings it has, the state of its electronics, the brand of pickups, whether it's been banged up, refurbished, played since the 1970's or fresh from the factory—know that the instrument you hold, regardless of its brand and model, is a unique piece of musical equipment. That's pretty darn special.

CHAPTER III

How to Hold a Bass Guitar

Quite different from classical guitar, or any bass instrument in an orchestra, the bass guitar has several ways of being held and there's no one way that's absolutely correct. The important thing is whether the player is *comfortable*, which definitely has an effect on sound quality.

That being said, the usual ways of playing a bass guitar are standing up or sitting down.

Practicing Seated

Most of the time practicing by yourself will probably be done sitting down. It's also probably easier to master technique while sitting down than standing up, as it will perhaps help you be more patient (something very important when starting out).

If you're right-handed, the typical way to hold a bass is to rest it upon your right thigh with the back of the body close to your stomach and chest. Then, your left hand will be holding the neck and your right forearm resting over the body. Most basses have a slight slope on the body precisely so you can rest your forearm there. If you're left-handed, simply inverse this position: bass on the left thigh, right hand holding the neck and left hand plucking the strings.

This is a basic position for holding a bass guitar. Even if it's your hands and fingers doing most of the work, it's important that your entire body holds the bass properly so that you have sufficient stability and a comfortable stance to play with.

Practicing Standing Up

Playing a bass while standing is fairly similar! To get started, all you need is a strap which you can attach to the strap holders on the body of your bass. Once the strap is in place, simply put it over your head so that it goes around your body.

It's important to make sure that the strap isn't twisted when you put it on, as this can cause discomfort while playing.

Another thing to keep in mind is the position of your wrists while holding the bass. It's important to keep them straight to avoid fatigue and ensure that you're holding the instrument correctly.

You can check out the image to get an idea of proper wrist alignment while playing a bass standing up.

Different styles of holding the bass can be seen among famous bassists. For example, Geddy Lee holds his bass at a height aligned with his navel, with the strap resting straight over his left shoulder and the cable secured between the strap and its attachment to the bass.

Carlos Dengler and Duff McKagan also hold their basses at a similar height, aligning the edge of the bass with their navels. Jaco Pastorius, on the other hand, holds his bass lower, with the edge of the instrument almost touching the ground. You can check out images of different artists to see the different heights and styles in which the bass can be held.

Just remember to keep your wrists straight and take breaks as needed to avoid fatigue. That being said, it's completely OK for you to experiment with your bass height in order to look how you want to look. It's called style—and after all, it's an essential part of playing music too!

ABSOLUTE BASS-ICS

Walking you through the simple essentials of tuning your bass and reading music.

CHAPTER IV

Tuning

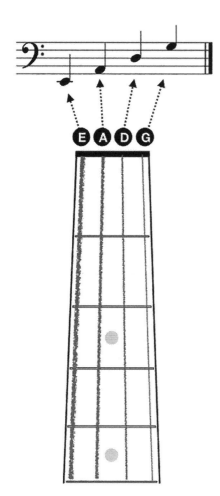

And now back to some technical stuff! With any stringed instrument, tuning is an essential step you'll want to do before you even consider playing a lick. This, and I can't stress this enough, is to the benefit of both yourself and everyone around you.

Nobody likes an out-of-tune player, so it's best to get this out of the way before we even begin playing. And don't worry— it's extremely simple!

First of all, you need to know what notes to tune your strings to. Here's a picture of your bass guitar neck viewed from the front, showing all four strings and the note (or 'pitch') each string should produce.

Moving from left to right (or from thickest string to thinnest string) we can see that the four strings are tuned **E A D G**. Hopefully easy enough remember without having to refer to this page constantly! But if not, try a mnemonic — something like "**E**lvis **A**lways **D**anced **G**reat," or "**E**very **A**ngry **D**og **G**rowls." You've probably got a better imagination than me, so make up your own!

These notes have also been displayed here on a conventional music stave above the neck picture. Don't worry if you don't read music (that's not important at this point), but notice how they're exactly evenly spaced? This is something that's going to come in very handy later on during this chapter...

Physically tuning the bass guitar simply involves turning those **tuning pegs** clockwise or counter-clockwise to alter the pitch of the string.

But how do you discover what pitch the string is making when you pluck it? You've basically got four options:

Get an Electronic Tuner

Quite possibly the greatest electronic aid for bass guitarists since the coffee machine was invented. A reliable electronic tuner is nearly as essential as a guitar strap when it comes to "kit you can't do without."

Most electronic tuners will show the name of the note being played on a display, usually in the center of a meter or dial that tells you if you're just *below* or just *above* the exact pitch. You want your **E A D** and **G** strings to each show dead-center on that dial.

Here you can see the three main types of electronic tuner:

- **Clip-on tuner**. This device clips onto the headstock of your bass and senses the note being played from the strings' vibration through the whole instrument. It can't be distracted by sound from any other source, making it very reliable. Best of all, you can pick these things up for a couple of dollars!

- ✓ **Portable electronic tuner**. These gadgets are larger than the clip-on devices, and normally give you the option of either plugging your bass directly in (meaning no distraction from other noises) OR using a built-in microphone to listen to the note being played. Small enough to fit in your pocket or easily tuck inside your instrument case.

- ✓ **Pedal tuner**. Also known as a "stage tuner". An essential piece of gigging equipment — run a cable from your bass to the tuner, then run a second cable from the tuner to your amp. The pedal is a switch that turns the tuner on and off, and it can usually be set to mute the sound going to your amp while you're tuning. (Let's be honest, your audience doesn't need to hear THAT...)

As long as you keep up with the batteries inside your tuner, this is undoubtedly the most accurate and probably most convenient method of getting (and staying) in tune.

Use an App

Anyone reading this almost certainly has access to a smartphone or tablet, which means you may potentially have a tuner in your pocket right now. Since we do everything on our phone these days anyway (you might even be reading this book on your phone!), why not also use it to tune our instrument?

The enormous range of tuning apps for iOS, Android, Windows, macOS and other devices increases every week, and I find it's usually worth having one of these available—*even if you already own an electronic tuner*. After all, why wouldn't you install a backup? Especially if you can download it for free.

Similarly, there are a number of free websites out there to help bass players tune up, both by playing notes on demand for you to hear as a reference point, AND by using your device's built-in microphone to listen to the notes you're playing.

Tune to a Keyboard

From this point on you need to rely on your ears. Don't worry — it's a lot easier than you might think!

If you have access to a piano (which ideally should itself be correctly tuned!) or electronic keyboard, then you already have the perfect

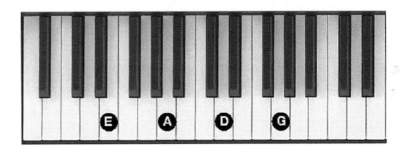

reference point to help you tune your bass.

This shows you how to find the correct notes on the keyboard to tune each string with. If you're lucky enough to have a full-size 88-key piano/keyboard then even better; make sure you're using the notes at the bottom end (left-hand side) of the instrument. Simply play the note on the keyboard and adjust the tuning peg of your bass string to match it.

Relative Tuning

Otherwise known as "tuning your bass to itself." Yes, this is actually possible—but ONLY if you know that one of your bass strings is already perfectly in tune.

Here's another image of your bass guitar neck from the front, showing the first 5 frets. The **A**, **D** and **G** strings are indicated right at the top of the neck, but notice how the same notes are also shown down at the 5th fret on different strings?

Assuming that your **E** string (thickest string, on the left) is perfectly in tune, then when you play it at the 5th fret, the note produced is an **A**. Put simply, if the notes sound identical then your **A** string should also be perfectly in tune.

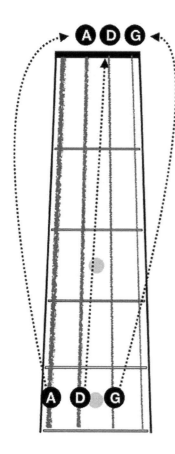

If they don't sound identical then adjust the tuning peg on the **A** string until the pitches match up. You might feel a strange wobble through the body of the bass (and you'll definitely hear it through an amplifier) if the pitches are REALLY close but not quite matched up—this is an oscillation caused by the dissonance between the **E** string's **A** note and whatever happened to the **A** string's pitch. Isn't physics cool!?

As demonstrated by the arrows in the image, this method can be used to tune all the strings on your bass:

E string played at 5th fret = open **A** string

A string played at 5th fret = open **D** string

D string played at 5th fret = open **G** string

And Finally... Use Our Tuning Track

Yup, if all else fails then take a listen to Track 1 and tune to that!

CHAPTER V

Theory 101: Introduction to TAB

Anyone beginning to learn a musical instrument from scratch will usually need to learn how to read music for that instrument. This idea has terrified newbies for years! .' Luckily, bass players are afforded a nice workaround to this problem...

Bass Tablature, or "**TAB**" for short, is a fantastically simple way of writing and reading music. It's basically a graphical representation of your bass neck, as I will now demonstrate:

Have a look at this image of the headstock and first few frets of a bass neck, seen from the perspective of someone actually holding the instrument ready to play.

And compare it with this empty bass TAB stave.

String 1 **G**
String 2 **D**
String 3 **A**
String 4 **E**

Notice the similarity?

The four lines on the TAB represent the four strings on a bass guitar from the player's viewpoint, with the **low E** string at the bottom and the **high G** at the top. So whenever you look at a bass TAB stave written down, you're also kinda looking at the strings of your own bass as it sits on your knee or strapped to your body.

What a great idea! And it's certainly not a new idea—Lute tablature (painstakingly written out by monks on parchment) can be traced back to at least the 15th Century.

Actual written notes are also very simple in TAB. Numbers written on the lines tell you which number fret to play on each string (counting the frets upwards from the headstock), with a zero ("0") written for an open string. If there are no numbers on a string then you simply don't play that string. And you read it in exactly the same way as you read conventional notation, from left to right.

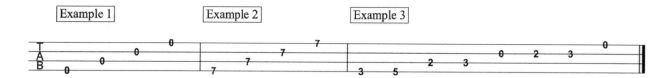

See how it works?

Example 1 shows the **E A D** and **G** strings (or strings 4, 3, 2 and 1 respectively) being played open, one after each other.

Example 2 shows the same thing, but with all four strings now being played at the 7th fret.

Example 3 shows a mixture of notes being played across all four strings, including a couple of open strings. If you actually try this out then you'll hear a G7 scale.

CHAPTER VI

Theory 102: Introduction to Rhythm

Since we're now familiar with how TAB works, I wouldn't blame you at this point for asking "So why do we need the normal music stave at all? Can't bass players just stick with TAB all the time?"

TAB is a brilliant invention, no doubt about that. And as you get better and better as a bassist, the advantages of writing music in this way will become even more obvious. One good example is that the bass guitar allows more than one way of playing the same note (the pitch of the open G string can also be found at three other places on the neck, for goodness sake!) so TAB eliminates any such ambiguity.

Although TAB is perfect for clearly defining exact pitch, what it can't sensibly do is show exact **rhythm**—and rhythm is absolutely critical to good bass playing.

Look back to **The Role Of The Bass Player** in **Chapter 1:** "the bass player in any sort of ensemble holds both the harmonic base and rhythmic base on his or her shoulders." Wise words if I do say so myself! But how about some words from the legendary Bootsy Collins (bassist for Parliament-Funkadelic, James Brown, George Clinton, Snoop Dogg, the list goes on...), who said:

"The drums are the police, but the bass is the law."

What a statement! And he's absolutely correct too. Yes, the drums are an integral part of what we'd consider 'the rhythm section' in most bands, but the rhythm thrown out by the bass is generally what the drummer should be following and building upon.

Rhythm is very clearly spelled out for musicians in conventional notation. This is done simply by adding different kinds of tails and beams to notes, sometimes by using white instead of black notes, and by loads of other symbols and tricks that lets the musician know exactly how long each note should be played.

Conventional notation also tells us when NOT to play, thanks to symbols known as "rests".

A simple rhythm tree is the best way to show you the relationship between all the notes and all the rests.

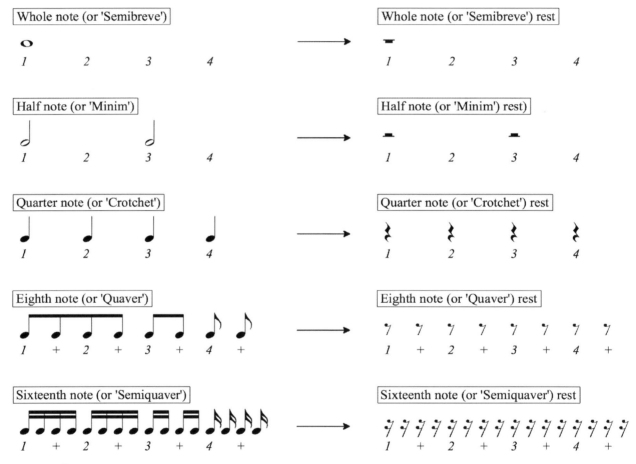

❷ All these different rhythms are conveniently related to each other; I've numbered the Quarter note beats under every example to make this clearer. You can see that a Whole note is played for the same length of time as two Half notes; a Half note lasts for the same duration as two Quarter notes, and so on. You get the idea!

- Every kind of rhythm can be shown as a note or a rest. And rests have exactly the same relationship between their durations as notes do. Four Quarter note rests would mean you'd stay silent for the same duration as one Whole note rest.

- That line stemming from the Half, Quarter, Eighth and Sixteenth notes is known as a "tail".

- Notice how the Eighth and Sixteenth notes are either joined together by "beams" (usually when there's more than one of them grouped up) or have "flags" (usually when they're by themselves).

A great way to get your head around the relationships between these rhythms is to tap out a continuous *1 2 3 4* quarter note rhythm with your foot. Maybe even say it out loud as you tap. Now try clapping the other rhythms out over the top. Just don't hurt yourself when you get to the Sixteenth notes...

It's when you imagine trying to add different kinds of tails to the numbers on a TAB stave that the problem starts to become obvious. Also imagine trying to write different colored numbers on a TAB stave at the same time. I'm sure the picture in your head looks pretty messy and difficult to read, and that's even before adding other more advanced rhythmic symbols and indicators. We need clear, readable music—not something that looks spat out of a broken Xerox machine...

The solution to this problem is to **write the same music in two different ways**, using conventional notation (showing rhythm AND pitch) along with TAB (showing precisely where to play on the neck of the bass). Let's try that with the TAB example from the last chapter.

Even without the beat numbering above the music, you can see how clearly the rhythm is now displayed. This is also a good opportunity to explain a couple of other very useful features of conventional notation that will help you play your TAB more accurately:

- Music is usually divided into **measures** or **bars** — small sections that contain a fixed amount of beats.

- These different measures are divided up on both the conventional and TAB staves by vertical **bar lines**. You can also see the **final bar line** at the end of this example,represented by one thin and one thick line. This is almost always how the end of a piece of music is indicated.

- The **time signature** is displayed at the start of the music on the conventional stave — 4/4 in this case. The top number specifies exactly how many beats are in each measure, while the bottom number indicates the type of beat. So music written in 4/4 time will hold four quarter note beats per bar, and music written in 6/8 time will hold six eighth note beats in each bar.

- The beats in each measure **MUST** equal the time signature, no matter what actual beats or rests are used. This makes the music much simpler to follow by grouping notes and rests into equal length batches, so the musician can easily anticipate just how long each batch will last.

- Some of the tails on the quarter notes point in different directions;that's simply to make them fit neatly inside the five lines on the conventional stave and doesn't affect the rhythm at all.

And with that short crash course in TAB and rhythm, I'd say that's all the music theory we need to concern ourselves with for now. It's time to start making some noise!

THE LOW-DOWN

These strings are made for plucking, and that's just what we'll do. (Let's learn how to pick.)

CHAPTER VII

Picking Through Basic Rhythms

So you've tuned your bass, you know how to hold the thing (whether standing or sitting), and we're about ready to try reading through some TAB. But first of all, let's just think about how to actually play this 4-stringed monster.

The first and most important rule for both hands and arms (heck, this should apply to your entire body) is to **STAY RELAXED**.

I apply this rule to just about every aspect of my life to be honest, but it's of particular benefit when playing a musical instrument. If you think about it, playing a musical instrument is actually a pretty unnatural thing for the human body to attempt. Either as a result of intelligent design or evolution, we're built to run around, gather food, hit other humans (maybe even hit on other humans if the mood is right), etc. We're not built to drive vehicles, sit in office chairs for hours on end, roller-skate, break dance, or repeatedly jam our fingers against thick metal wires attached to a heavy lump of wood.

Trust me: tension is your enemy when playing the bass. Finding a comfortable playing position for both hands is the key to making the whole experience better.

The second and nearly-as-important-as-the-first-and-most-important-rule is to **TRIM YOUR FINGERNAILS**.

This isn't an attack on your beauty regime I promise. But you will be using the tips of your fingers to either pick thick metal strings, or to push thick metal strings against a lump of wood. If there's any fingernail getting in the way of you performing those actions then I can guarantee it's going to have a negative effect on the sound (not to mention what all that metal is gonna do to your fingernails).

Hey, there's still plenty of ways to look glamorous and stylish while playing bass! (Remember, style is an essential part of music.) But if you want to actually enjoy learning this thing, I'm afraid the long nails have got to go.

Picking hand technique

There are a few different ways to pluck, twang, strike or tickle a bass guitar string into vibrating and making noise. We're going to focus on **fingerstyle,** by far the most common method, which allows you maximum control, and usually lets you play faster than the other techniques.

Your basic starting position is shown here:

- ✓ The forearm should be positioned comfortably somewhere over the top edge of the instrument.

- ✓ The hand should be loosely hanging down in front of the strings.

- ✓ Fingers should also be loosely hanging down in front of the strings. Try to keep them straight, not curled.

- ✓ Rest your thumb gently on the top of the pickup — this provides the best 'home position' for your picking hand.

Now gently rest the fleshy part of the end of your **index (i)** finger on the **E** string (**string 4**), and have your **middle (m)** finger standing by. We're going to try picking the exercise below, just on this string.

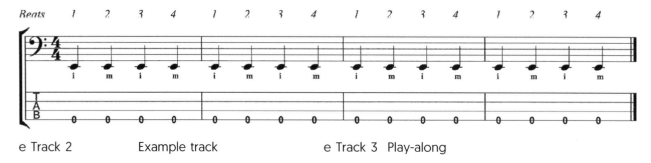

e Track 2   Example track   e Track 3   Play-along

Pay close attention to the beats numbered above the stave, and the fingering information beneath each **Quarter note**:

- ✓ Play each note EXACTLY on the beat

- ✓ Alternate between the index and middle fingers as you play

Alternating between two fingers will probably feel weird at first, but it's absolutely worth building this muscle memory very early on.

The trick you're learning here is the simplest, but one of the most important for a bassist: keeping things in time.

Go ahead and have a practice along with the tracks! Be sure to listen carefully to the beat of the drums to help you, sticking evenly to the speed (no slowing down or speeding up!). Notice how the bass drum hits on beats 1 & 3, and the snare hits on beats 2 & 4—this is a very common feature in popular music.

Now we'll have a play around on the **A** string (**string 3**) in a slightly different way. Move your **index (i)** finger down to rest on the **A** string, keeping your thumb in position rested against the top of the pickup for the moment, and try picking through this exercise.

e Track 4   Example track   e Track 5 Play-along

- ✓ Every **Quarter note** is separated by a **Quarter note Rest**, both of which last for one beat (as indicated above the stave).

- ✓ For the notes, pick the **A** string with your **index (i)** finger, and let it come to rest against the **E** string.

- ✓ For the rests, move your **index** finger back to rest on the **A** string—this will mute the note (stopping the string vibrating) and get you ready to pick the next note.

- ✓ The dots on the final barline are telling you to **Repeat** the entire section. So play the whole thing through twice.

Using your fingers to mute the strings is just as important a skill as picking them, so try to make sure the sound you're making here matches the playing on the example track. Both the notes AND the rests should last for one beat each.

If you can master this exercise using just the **index** finger, try it again using the **middle** finger in exactly the same way. Maybe even try alternating between the two—just don't forget the rests!

39

Let's now try using two strings, with a different finger on each, playing through 8 bars of very simple rock. Your thumb can stay anchored on the top of the pickup throughout this exercise.

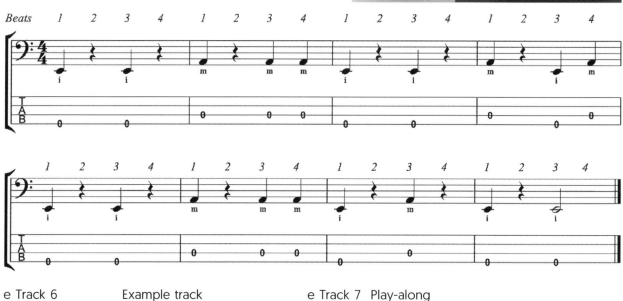

e Track 6   Example track   e Track 7 Play-along

- ✔ Your **index (i)** finger is now in control of picking and muting just the **E** string (**string 4**), while your **middle (m)** finger is doing exactly the same on the **A** string (**string 3**) .

- ✔ When you pick the **A** string, allow your **middle** finger to come to rest against the **E** string (even if your index finger is already resting there). This is good practice for muting lower strings as you play higher strings, and something that we'll be talking about a LOT later on in this book.

- There's a good mix of both **Quarter notes** and **Quarter note rests** in this tune—make sure you're playing (and muting) them all exactly where you should, and that they last for exactly the correct length!

- Notice that there's also a **Half note** right at the end of the exercise. This lasts for 2 beats — the same length as two Quarter notes added together.

Playing the **D** string (**string 2**) works much the same way as playing the **A** string, but it does require a slight change of position for your entire picking hand. Simply move your thumb down to rest on the **E** string when you're playing the **D** string.

You'll find that your picking hand will naturally become pretty mobile over time—and this is a good thing! Having an anchor point, whether it's on the pickup or any of the lower pitched strings, gives your hand and fingers a useful point of reference. It also means you naturally mute the lower strings that aren't being played, which stops them ringing out when you don't want them to.

Now for a test of picking stamina...

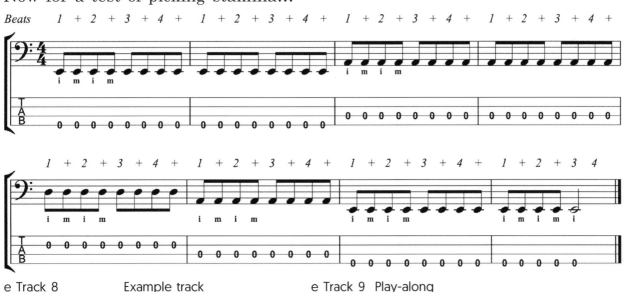

e Track 8   Example track   e Track 9 Play-along

- We're back to alternating our picking between the **index** and **middle** fingers (as indicated), but this time with **Eighth notes**. Whoa, things are getting faster! Don't forget that **Half note** at the end...

- Moving up the strings is actually pretty easy—let both the **index** and **middle** fingers come to rest against the **E** string after picking the **A**, and the **A** string after picking the **D**. This automatically mutes the string lower than the one being played.

- Slightly trickier is moving back down the strings from the **D** to the **A** and back to the **E**, purely because it's harder to mute the higher string you've just played but are now moving down from. This is where your fretting hand can help out; just lightly touch a finger against any string you don't want to hear ringing out.

This short rock exercise mixes up everything we've picked through so far:

e Track 10   Example track   e Track 11 Play-along

- You should be getting pretty confident with these different rhythms now, but check the example track to make sure you're playing them accurately!

- The rests in this exercise give you plenty of opportunity to cleanly mute strings before moving your fingers to the next one. Play through this a few times and experiment with muting using either your **ring** or **middle** finger. Or perhaps both at the same time if you feel like it.

✔ Teaching your hands and fingers new tricks like this means they'll soon be operating on automatic when it comes to picking your way around the strings.(That's **Muscle Memory**!)

We'll take a step back in terms of rhythm for this exercise, which counts as your first "proper" tune — a simple **12-bar blues**.

This is without a doubt the most popular structure ever used in popular music, with *thousands* of recorded songs produced in this form. It's a little weird to think that "Boom Boom" (John Lee Hooker) is identical in structure to "I Feel Good"(James Brown), "Ball & Biscuit" (The White Stripes) and "Still Haven't Found What I'm Looking For"(U2) —but there ya go.

Because it's a simple song (all you need is one hand to play it!), I won't make it *too* easy for you. There's no beat numbering or fingering information in this one, since I reckon you can figure that out for yourself!

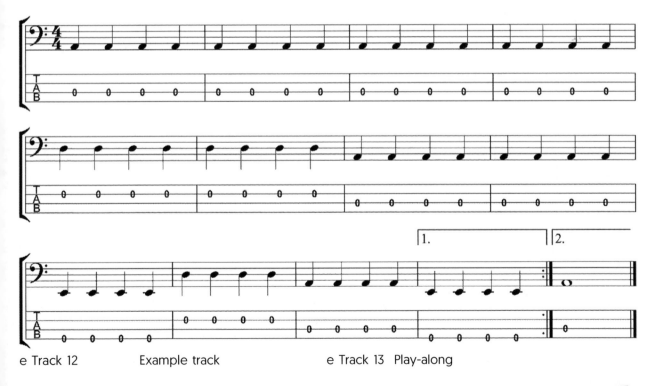

e Track 12   Example track   e Track 13 Play-along

43

- One new feature here is a **1ˢᵗ-time and 2ⁿᵈ-time bar** ending. This is simply a method of making the repeat section more interesting. Play through the first time, end on the bar marked **1°**, and go straight back to the start like the repeat sign tells you to. The second time around you should skip this bar and jump straight to the bar marked **2°**.

- This constant quarter note style of playing is known as a **Walking bass** line. These types of bass parts are a common feature in blues, jazz and many other genres and certainly don't need to stay on one note. Jazz bass in particular has a tendency to walk all over the place...

SIMPLE MOVEMENT

Getting your other hand working around the bass neck.

CHAPTER VIII

Moving Onto the Neck

There are some instruments that you can comfortably and easily play with one hand (Bugle, Tambourine, Kazoo, the list goes on…) but the bass guitar isn't one of them. So let's now look at adding your fretting hand into the mix and onto the neck of your bass.

Hand Technique

Unlike your picking hand, you should be using all four fingers to fret notes on the bass neck. These fingers are numbered as shown. Notice that your thumb doesn't have a number—it should be tucked away behind the bass neck and pressing against the wood.

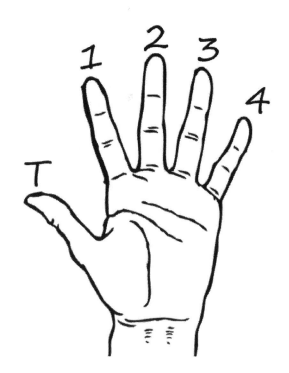

Once again, remember the first principle of a good playing position is to STAY RELAXED. I personally find the best way to start figuring out a "happy place" with your fretting hand/arm position is to try this:

Grip the neck of your bass with your fretting hand

Then...

Let your arm go completely limp from the shoulder down, so that it's hanging from the bass neck.

This should (hopefully) leave your arm in a completely natural position for playing. And if you're trying this trick while sitting down, don't make the mistake of resting your elbow on your knee. That's just lazy!

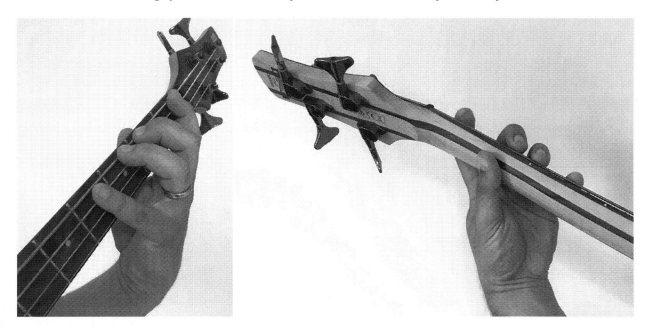

Your basic starting position is shown here:

- ✅ Your thumb should be placed on the back of the neck, roughly in the middle and somewhere behind fingers 1 and 2. Don't worry too much if it moves around while playing, just make sure it doesn't creep too far over the top of the neck or anywhere behind the headstock.

- ✅ Your fingers should be spaced out, ready to use finger 1 on the 1st fret, finger 2 on the 2nd fret, and so on.

- ✅ Strings should be fretted in the gaps *between* the actual frets, directly behind each fret if possible, and definitely NOT on the metal frets themselves.

- Use the tips of your fingers when fretting (as if your fingers are pointing straight down towards the strings) rather than the fleshy pads. You can actually apply more pressure this way.

It's pretty common for new players to try and avoid using fingers 3 and 4 when starting out. This is due to a combination of factors: your two smaller fingers are naturally weaker than fingers 1 and 2, and stretching all four fingers across the widely-spaced frets of a bass guitar isn't exactly comfortable.

But I *urge* you, I *beg* you—in fact, I *demand* of youthis one thing: **persevere!** Your ability to comfortably use all four fingers to fret notes will improve every time your practice; the strength of your fingers will gradually increase, the tips of your fingers will toughen up, and your body will generally adapt to these strange new demands you're making of it.

And remember that if things start hurting in any way, then STOP! Take a break. Let your arm relax and take a rest. Playing through the pain just isn't fun and can potentially result in an injury, which REALLY isn't fun. I'm trying to teach you here, not hurt you.

Let's start this whole fretting thing off by playing a little jazz bass. (I guess you could call this *swinging* into action! Wow, that was a bad joke...)

e Track 14   Example track   e Track 15 Play-along

- Since the rhythm here is mostly non-stop **Quarter notes**, this bass line is another example of a **Walking bass**.

- This exercise should really get your fretting-hand fingers working, although we're avoiding finger 4 at this early stage.

- Keep your fretting hand right at the bottom of the neck for this one (near the headstock), with finger 1 positioned over fret 1. This is known as **First position** (it naturally follows that positioning finger 1 ready over fret 2 is called **Second position**, and so on all the way up the neck...)

- Fingering for your fretting hand is labelled beneath the notes on the conventional stave. Since we're in **First position**, you can see that fingers 1, 2 and 3 conveniently play frets 1, 2 and 3.

- You're playing in first position over both the **E** string (**string 4**) and **A** string (**string 3**) but this is pretty simple—just move the fingers up and down strings. Make sure they stay on the right frets though!

- Fingering for your picking hand isn't included here as I'm confident you shouldn't need it. Just play through the exercise a few times to work out what works best for you. One thing to be aware of is muting the **A** string when moving to the **E** string. See if you can do it using either hand.

- Notice those symbols next to some of the notes on the conventional stave? They're called **Sharps** (♯), **Flats** (♭) and **Naturals** (♮) — otherwise referred to as **Accidentals**.

You'll only need to use fingers 1 and 3 on your fretting hand for this Reggae-inspired exercise:

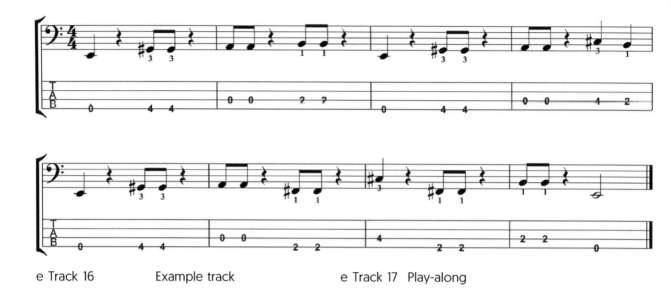

e Track 16   Example track   e Track 17 Play-along

- This exercise is based in the **Second position** over the **E** string (**string 4**) and **A** string (**string 3**), so keep finger 1 ready over fret 2.

- There's a real mix of **Quarter notes** and **Eighth notes** to test your rhythmic skills here. And don't forget the rests!

Fret Clinic

Are your notes sounding buzzy or muffled? The doctor will see you now...

When you fret a string on the neck of the bass and play the note, the ideal outcome is a clear, ringing tone. Unsurprisingly, this doesn't always happen at first. New bassists are still getting their bodies used to working with their instrument, muscle memory has yet to develop and become secure, fingers might take a while to toughen up, and this can lead to a few notes here and there sounding less than perfect.

DO NOT let any of this put you off! We can diagnose what's causing these problems easily enough.

- **Your fingers might not be holding the strings down firmly enough.** This is a common reason for notes to sound bad, simply because these heavy strings aren't that easy to hold down. Solve this by simply pressing harder (yeah, it's THAT obvious). Imagine that you're pinching the string against the fingerboard, between your thumb and your fretted finger. Make sure you're using the tips of your fingers rather than the pads. And remember, if it's hurting then take a break...

- ✓ **Your fingers are either too close to the fret wires, or actually ON the fret wires.** Remember, your fingers should be fretting the strings in the gaps *between* the frets. Pushing a string directly against the fret wire can cause anything from a buzz to a muffled tone, and even potentially push the string against the next fret along the fingerboard. This will absolutely cause your bass to erupt in flames and explode. Don't say I didn't warn you!!

- ✓ **Your fingernails are too long**. Bad news for any fans of manicures and fabulous acrylic nail art, but it's true. If the nails on your fretting hand are too long then they can either prevent your fingertips pressing the strings down properly, or simply get in the way of an already vibrating string and cause it to buzz. We mentioned this earlier on, but you were probably still in denial. Trim those suckers right now.

- ✓ **You're not doing anything wrong at all. (Meaning it's the bass causing the problem**.) Sometimes a tempermental instrument just needs a bit of TLC before it plays and sounds as it should. The way the strings pass over the neck (usually in terms of height) is referred to as the **Action** of the bass—and sometimes the strings could be set too low or too high, or there's a fret standing a little taller than the others, or there's too much/too little curve in the neck itself.

    - ✓ If you suspect any of this might be the case, then it's time to find a good guitar technician. For a nominal fee, they'll be happy to perform a **Setup** on your instrument, which can potentially make a $100 bass play and sound like a $1000 bass. Score!

OK, let's take it up a notch. We're going to avoid ANY open strings for the next few exercises, starting with some quick practical theory lessons.

What we have here is known as a **Major Scale** — C major in this example.

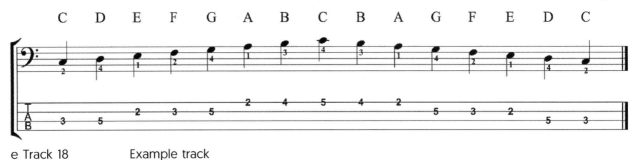

e Track 18   Example track

- Scales are incredibly useful to know, particularly for a bass player. They help you learn the "feel" of a certain **Key** (the group of notes or pitches that are used to form a song or piece of music). You're also training your fretting hand to remember the "shape" of the scale on the fretboard.

- Notice that this scale climbs up (**Ascending**) and then back down (**Descending**) through all the notes in the key of C major, which have been named for you.

- You should have your fretting hand ready in **Second position** to play this scale, even though it starts on the 3rd fret. The fingering has been marked for you on the conventional stave; all four fingers are being used here.

- Listen to the demo track of this one and have a go at it yourself. There's no need to play it in time (although keeping a steady pace is always good), but try to make sure you're using the right fingers!

52

And now to use that same scale in a short tune.

e Track 19   Example track   e Track 20   Play-along

- ✔ Start off with the fretting hand in second position again—you should be able to manage this exercise without any fingering guide, and you WILL need all four fingers!

- ✔ The dots written directly above or below the notes indicate that they should be played **Staccato**, meaning sharply detached or separated from other notes. This is a type of musical **Articulation,** but remember that it shouldn't affect the note length.

Many people think of the major scale as sounding "happy", including me! Comparatively, the **Minor scale** tends to sound more "sad". Have a play through this C minor to see what I mean.

e Track 21   Example track

- The differences between this C minor scale and the C major scale you tried before are caused by the **Flats** you can see on the conventional stave. These accidentals drop the pitch of the 3rd, 6th and 7th note of the major scale by one **Semitone,** the smallest change in pitch that's possible to play on most instruments. (Each fret on a bass is one semitone apart.)

- This C minor scale starts and ends on the same fret position as the C major, but you can see big differences in the way that it ascends and descends on the frets. Start this scale with your fretting hand in **Third position**—you'll only need fingers 1, 3 and 4. Fingering has been marked for you on the conventional stave.

- It's definitely worth practicing this one a few times (and again, don't worry too much about playing it in time) just to become familiar with the "shape" of the scale on the fretboard and the "feel" of the minor key. More popular songs have been written in the minor key than the major key throughout musical history—just about all **Blues** music for starters!

Let's try using this scale in a slow, sad waltz tune:

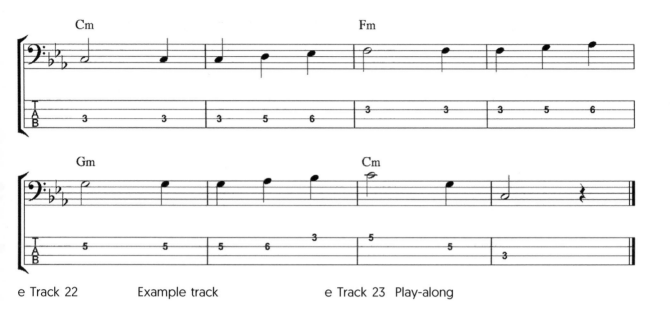

e Track 22   Example track   e Track 23 Play-along

- There's a completely new **Time signature** for you to try here. Remember that the top number indicates the number of beats per bar, and the bottom number shows the type of beat. So 3/4 means three quarter note beats per bar—a classic waltz feel.

- Beats are numbered in the first two bars to help you secure the waltz feel, and the rhythm stays the same through the rest of the exercise.

- Notice the **Flats** grouped together at the start of each line on the conventional stave? This is known as a **Key Signature** and basically tells you to use the indicated accidental throughout the music, meaning you don't need to write individual flats or sharps by each note. A key signature tells the musician—you guessed it!—what **Key** the music is in.

- I've also included the name of the **Chord** used in each bar, written above the stave.

HARMONY

Understanding how your bass playing works around the music.

CHAPTER IX

Basic Harmony

What is a Chord?

To answer this very important question we're going to dip our toes into a tiny bit more theory. Just our toes though—not a whole foot. Or leg. And we're certainly not diving in head first...

Put simply, a **Chord** is more than one note/pitch played at the same time.

We mentioned that scales are useful for learning to play in a certain **Key**. Well, so are chords, since all keys have both a scale AND a chord.

- ✓ The scale is usually used to play the **Melody**. This is typically the vocal line and things like a guitar or saxophone solo in a tune.

- ✓ The chord is usually used to provide the **Harmony**. This is a combination of notes played by the piano, guitar, or other background instrumentation that supports the melody.

You might be wondering how any of this applies to the bass guitar. Let's be honest, it's not that common to find a bass solo leading the melody in a song; bass guitars usually play individual notes—strumming a chord on this instrument would sound like a murky mess!

But think back to what we've already said about the role of the bass player: providing the foundation of the harmony and rhythm in an ensemble of musicians. A bassline can establish the feel of both the beat AND the entire key without any other instrument playing a single note. The waltz you've just played does exactly that using the C minor scale.

The ability to pick out notes from both a scale AND a chord in whatever key you play in is therefore a very useful skill indeed. So let's look at how chords work, shall we?

Here's the scale of C major again, but shown in a different way:

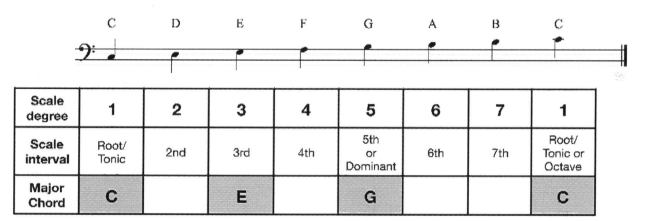

Scale degree	1	2	3	4	5	6	7	1
Scale interval	Root/ Tonic	2nd	3rd	4th	5th or Dominant	6th	7th	Root/ Tonic or Octave
Major Chord	C		E		G			C

❷ The conventional stave at the top shows the actual **Scale**, with the individual notes named.

❷ The top row in the table beneath the stave shows which **Degree** of the scale each note represents. Major and Minor scales all feature seven degrees. See how working your way up the scale from C to C gets you back to the Root again?

❷ The middle row of the table shows which **Interval** of the scale each note represents. Notice that intervals work in a pretty similar way to degrees, but there are particular words to describe some of them. The 1st degree is always the **Root** note of the key (sometimes called the **Tonic**), and the 5th degree can also be referred to as the

Dominant (you'll see how useful and common the 5th is in bass playing later on). And working your way up the scale brings you back to the root note, but this time it sounds an **Octave** higher.

● The bottom row of the table shows which degrees or intervals from this C major scale make up the notes used in a C major **Chord**. A major chord features three notes: the root/tonic, the 5th/dominant, and the **Major 3rd**. A three-note chord is otherwise known as a **Triad**.

Arpeggios

So if strumming a chord on a bass isn't going to work, how do you play one then? Simple. Break it up into a sequence of notes by playing an **Arpeggio**, also known as a **Broken chord**.

Think of the way a harp sounds when chords are being performed, one note plucked at a time—even the word arpeggio literally means "harp-like". You could even think of it as a chord broken into a very simple scale.

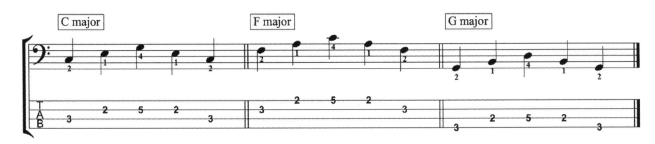

e Track 24   Example track

● You should have your fretting hand ready in **Second position** to play these arpeggios, even though they start on the **3rd** fret. The fingering has been marked for you on the conventional stave. Notice how this is the same position (and even the same fretting for just these three notes) that you used on the major scale? All you're doing here is playing a sort of "trimmed down" version of that scale.

✅ Listen to the demo track of these arpeggios and try them out by yourself. Try to keep a steady pace and make sure you're using the right fingers! The target here would be to play each individual arpeggio smoothly on repeat (bass guitar parts tend to do that a LOT).

There's probably no better practical example of arpeggios in action on the bass guitar than playing through a 12-bar blues. Let's try it in two different ways:

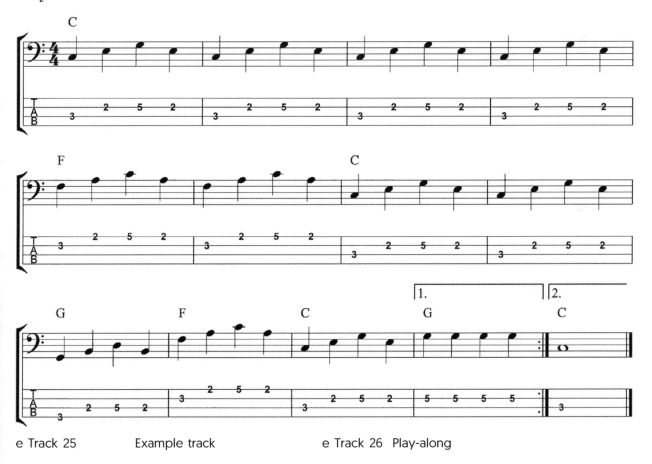

e Track 25   Example track   e Track 26 Play-along

✅ This is a *very* simple walking bass (almost all quarter notes and no rests) that just uses the three arpeggios we've looked at.

- Chord names have been included above the conventional stave again; this is something you'll see from now on in this book. When written above the stave in this way, they're known as **Chord symbols**. In this case they're helpful for reminding you which arpeggio is being used in each bar, but there's a few other features you'll need to know...

- Notice how they're not written above every bar? It's not actually necessary; the chord symbol indicates the key being used in the tune, and that key remains the same until the next chord symbol changes it.

- A chord symbol by itself (i.e. just "C") indicates a **Major** chord. If it was written as "Cm" then this would indicate a **Minor** chord.

- The key thing to focus on here is keeping the rhythm completely smooth and in time, with nice clean notes throughout—particularly when you change between strings! Use whatever method feels the most comfortable with your picking hand fingers. (I tend to use just my index finger on the lower string and my middle finger on the upper string, for each individual broken chord.)

Our next example adds a **Swing** to the rhythm—another very common feature of 12-bar blues bass lines, especially when actually playing the blues (or jazz, rock'n'roll, boogie-woogie and loads of other styles).

The simplest explanation of how to swing a rhythm is that the quarter-note beats are subdivided into eighth notes, which are then alternately lengthened and shortened. 1:1 becomes 2:1, where the total length of 2:1 remains within the 1:1 pulse...AAAAARGH!!!! That wasn't simple at all!

A better method is to try singing it. I'm gonna get a little mathematical and weird on you here, but bear with me...

Let "**Doo**" = One **Eighth note** beat

Now sing "**Doo Doo Doo Doo Doo Doo Doo Doo**" at a nice even tempo.

You've just performed a bar of music with a **Straight rhythm**.

Now, let "**Dum**" = One **Quarter note** beat, and let "**Di**" = One **Eighth note** beat.

Now sing "**Dum Di Dum Di Dum Di Dum Di**" kinda the same speed you just sung the Doo's.

Hey, presto—you've just performed a bar of music with a **Swing Rhythm!**

Hopefully no-one was watching you do that. If they were, explain it was for science…

An even better method is to illustrate it. Look at this diagram. You can see that, although the eighth notes are written normally, they should sound like a quarter note followed by an eighth note squeezed into the space of one quarter note beat.

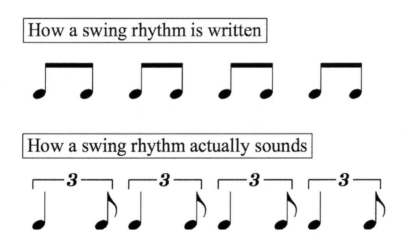

No wonder swing has been called "the most debated word in jazz." When jazz performer Cootie Williams was asked to define it, he joked: "Define it? I'd rather tackle Einstein's theory!"

Better still, have a listen to the example track for this swung 12-bar blues...

e Track 27   Example track   e Track 28 Play-along

- Don't let the mix of quarter and eighth notes (and even the occasional eighth note rest) put you off too much—each bar in this example uses EXACTLY the same arpeggio, played in EXACTLY the same position, as the previous exercise.

- Also don't let the mix of quarter and eighth notes confuse your approach to the whole "swing" rhythm idea we're using here. Remember that you're only swinging the eighth notes; the quarter notes are played normally.

- And while we're on that subject, when you see an eighth note rest followed by an eighth note, they're swung in the same way as two eighth notes next to each other! You have to admit, Cootie Williams was a wise, wise man... (see previous page!)

- ✓ You also only get two different rhythm patterns for most of the exercise, alternating each bar, which only changes in the 1° and 2° bars at the end.

- ✓ Listening to the cymbal on the backing track will help you target that swing rhythm feel.

All major scales/keys have their major arpeggios, so naturally the same is true for minor scales/keys.

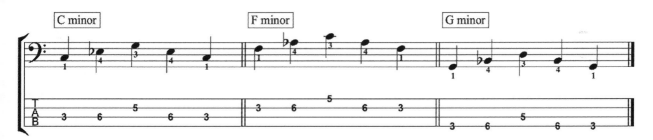

e Track 29   Example track

- ✓ Just like the major scale diagram you saw that explained how the major chord works, a minor chord and arpeggio have a very similar construction. You need the root/tonic and the fifth/dominant, but this time we add a **Minor third** rather than a major third. That's basically achieved by taking a major third and flattening it (note those accidentals on the conventional stave).

- ✓ See how those **Flat** symbols (♭) only appear once during each bar on the conventional stave? They work in a similar way to chord symbols; if you place a sharp or flat on a note within a bar, then all other occurrences of that note will stay sharpened or flattened until the next bar. For example, if you want to write four E-flats in a row then the flat symbol only needs to go by the first one.

- Start this scale with your fretting hand in **Third position;** you'll only need fingers 1, 3 and 4, as indicated on the conventional stave. Once again, notice this is the same position (and even the same fretting for just these three notes) that you used on the minor scale?

- Listen to the demo track of these arpeggios and try them out by yourself. Again, try to keep a steady pace, make sure you're using the right fingers, and see if you can smoothly play them on repeat.

Remember our swung 12-bar blues? Here it is again! Sort of...

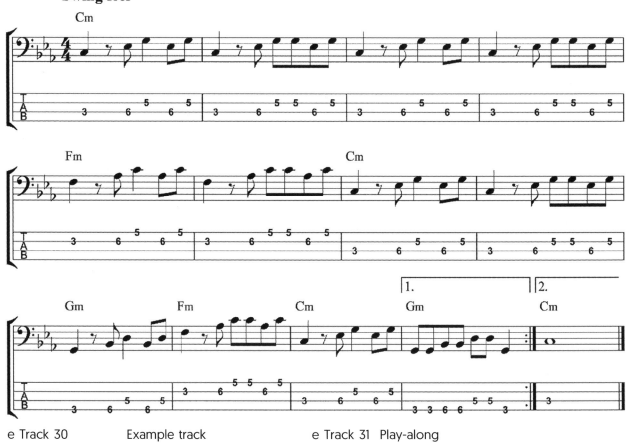

e Track 30   Example track   e Track 31 Play-along

- This exercise is actually an exact mirror of the major swing 12 bar exercise you tried before, only now it uses the minor arpeggio instead. So remember to start in third position!

✓ See how it "feels" completely different? That cheerful feeling of the major scale has immediately become a little more depressed with the use of a minor key.

Staying within our minor arpeggios, but stepping a long way away from both 12-bar blues and swing rhythms, here's a short Latin exercise for you to dance your way through!

e Track 32   Example track   e Track 33 Play-along

✓ There's quite a bit for you to process here, so I've added correct fretting-hand fingering throughout. Don't be scared; remember we're still purely using the notes from standard minor arpeggios, just played in a slightly different order. Stick to the fretting hand fingering that's written and you should have no difficulty.

✓ When it comes to your picking hand, I'd suggest index finger on the lower string and middle finger on the upper string; this should make it easier to silence each string for the rests when you need to—and DO try to make those rests stand out!

● This rhythm features a musical device called **Syncopation,** otherwise known as playing on the "off-beat" or "anticipating the next beat"a very common feature in Latin style music. I've numbered the beats in each bar throughout this exercise to help you navigate this concept, but I'd definitely suggest listening to the demo track so you get a better idea of how the rhythm should feel.

CONTROL

Developing the way your fingers keep the sound of your bass in check.

CHAPTER X

String Control Basics

Remember earlier on when I said that **Fingerstyle** is the method of playing a bass guitar that gives you maximum control? It's time to focus on one major aspect of that level of control: **Muting**. One of the most difficult areas of bass guitar technique, particularly as a beginner, isn't so much getting noise out of the instrument. No, it's actually shutting the darn thing up!

Why would that be important? Well, let's learn a little bit more about the fabulous bass guitar and how it produces sound.

The solid-bodied electric guitar was truly one of the greatest developments in instrument design, allowing much greater string resonance due to the heavier wooden construction (never mind the addition of electronics) compared with hollow-bodied electric or purely acoustic instruments.

The late, great Leo Fender was absolutely central to this step forward in the early 1950's with the Telecaster and Stratocaster electric guitars. He then brilliantly applied the same design principles a couple of years later to his Precision Bass, thereby inventing a completely new musical instrument/discipline in one stroke! Mr. Fender, we salute you.

But let's consider one *possible* drawback. A bass guitar is bigger than an electric guitar,meaning it uses a lot more wood—so the potential for string resonance is much greater. The strings themselves are much thicker than those found on electric guitars and cover a much greater distance between the headstock and bridge, so they naturally vibrate for much longer,either when actually played or when vibrating from sympathetic resonance when you play a different string.

Throw all these factors together and the risk of unintended low frequency rumble from your bass becomes very clear. And if you're using an amp with more than 50w of power then it will become clearer still.

This is why the art of string muting needs to be second nature to a bass guitarist. You must ensure that the notes you're playing aren't muddled by the ringing of notes you've already played on other strings, or other notes ringing out from strings you weren't even intending to play.

The fingers on both your hands will need to learn to think for themselves (**Muscle memory** in action again), allowing your brain the freedom to concentrate on more important matters. You know, things like grooving in the right key, playing in time, and bullying your drummer. The exercises in this chapter are going to help you do just that...

Our first couple of exercises focus very deeply on technique. We're playing basic quarter notes and just moving in simple intervals of a **5**th, up and down the strings—but it's the way you play these intervals that will secure good muting practice into the way your fingers work.

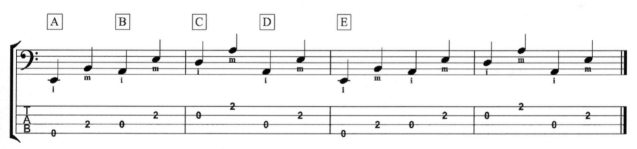

e Track 34   Example track

We only want to hear the strings being played ONE AT A TIME, so make absolutely sure you stick to the picking hand fingering indicated. Let's move through the technique here in detail:

- **Point A (start of the first bar)**: Keep your thumb anchored on the pickup. Pick the **E** string with your **index finger**. Then, after picking the **A** string with your **middle finger**, let it come to rest against the **E** string—this should automatically mute the **E** string.

- **Point B**: Move your thumb and anchor it on the **E** string. Pick the **A** string with your **index finger** and let it come to rest on the **E** string. (You've now muted the **E** string in 2 different ways!) Then, after picking the **D** string with your **middle finger**, let it come to rest against the **A** string. This should automatically mute the **A** string.

- **Point C (start of the second bar)**: Move your thumb and anchor it on the **A** string, but also lean it slightly against the **E** string; this means that the thumb is automatically muting two different strings. Pick the **D** string with your **index finger** and let it come to rest on the **A** string. Then, after picking the **G** string with your **middle finger**, let it come to rest against the **D** string—this should automatically mute the **D** string.

- **Point D**: This is the tricky bit. Do all of this simultaneously: Move your thumb and anchor it on the **E** string, pick the **A** string with your **index finger** (letting it come to rest on the **E** string), AND lightly mute the **G** string with your **middle finger**. Then use that **middle finger** again to pick the **D** string and let it come to rest against the **A** string. This should automatically mute the **A** string.

- **Point E (start of the third bar)**: These next two bars are a repeat of the first two—but remember you've just played two different strings before starting out, and they need to be muted! So treat this the same way as **Point D**: Simultaneously move your thumb and anchor it on the pickup, pick the **E** string with your **index finger**, AND lightly mute the **D** string with your **middle finger**. Then use that **middle finger** again to pick the **A** string and let it come to rest against the **E** string—this should automatically mute the **E** string.

✓ Go back to **Point B** and repeat!

It doesn't matter which fingers you use on your fretting hand for this exercise, but one thing you might want to experiment with is using a fretting-hand finger to mute the higher string at **Point D** and **E**, rather than the middle finger of your picking hand.

Experimentation is absolutely going to benefit you when practicing muting— and if you can develop your own preferences and technique that works, then good for you!

Here we're trying the exact same thing, but moving things up to the **Third position**.

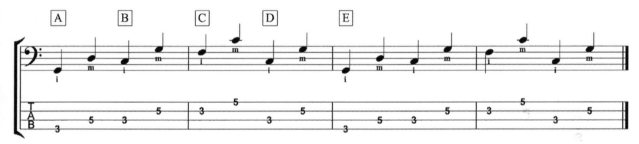

e Track 35   Example track

✓ Use exactly the same point-by-point technique that I detailed in the last exercise; it works identically across the strings in terms of the picking hand, but this time alternate between finger 1 (lower string) and finger 3 (higher string) on your fretting hand.

✓ This is another good opportunity to experiment with using your fretting-hand fingers to assist with the muting. You can manage this by keeping a light touch on the string after you've actually finished fretting the note. It'll take some practice!

Getting both hands to work together in this way kinda feels like patting your head and rubbing your stomach at the same time (anyone else remember trying that in kindergarten?), but you've definitely learned to coordinate complicated activities with both hands before now. Typing or using a knife and fork are two good examples...

Your head should be buzzing with muting technique ideas at this point, so let's try them out in a Country-style 12-bar blues:

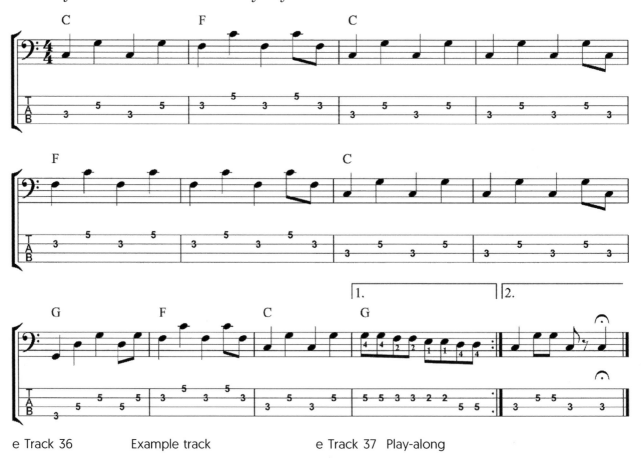

e Track 36   Example track   e Track 37 Play-along

● We're staying within the arpeggios used earlier for most of this tune, but mainly bouncing between the root/tonic and the 5th. This is a common bass playing technique for many different genres, but it absolutely dominates the bass lines used in country music. If you're a fan of Johnny Cash then this exercise will immediately sound familiar!

- Stick with the picking hand techniques you covered in the last two exercises, with the index finger playing the lower string, the middle finger covering the upper (including the muting when moving back down), and keeping your thumb position as mobile as it needs to be. I haven't put any fingering guidelines in the music; finding your own comfortable place should be pretty easy to do—just keep in mind that we only want to hear one note at a time!

- Your fretting hand can stay in second position for this whole exercise (mostly using finger 2 on the 3rd fret and finger 4 on the 5th fret). A good challenge would be to try using third position for the majority of the 12-bar (finger 1 on the 3rd fret and finger 3 on the 5th fret), shifting down to second position just to play the 1° bar as written. Changing positions while playing is something that bass players frequently do, and it's good to start practicing this early on.

- The symbol over the final quarter note in the 2° bar is called a **Fermata**—more commonly referred to as a **Pause**. Hold that final note for a little longer than normal, just for dramatic effect!

Right, time to get back to the technical exercises. At this point I'm gonna turn up the pressure a little by chopping those quarter notes into eighth notes...

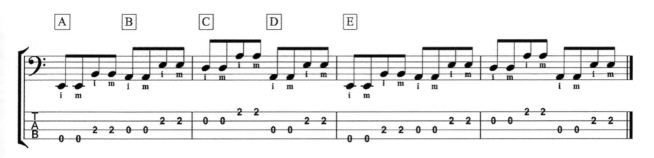

e Track 38   Example track

Once again we're only aiming to hear strings played ONE AT A TIME, so stick with the picking hand fingering written on the conventional stave.

- **Point A (start of the first bar)**: Keep your thumb anchored on the pickup. Pick the **E** string with your **index** then **middle finger**. Then do the same on the **A** string, letting both fingers come to rest against the **E** string and muting it.

- **Point B**: Move your thumb and anchor it on the **E** string. Pick the **A** string with your **index** then **middle finger**. Then do the same on the **D** string, letting both fingers come to rest against the **A** string and muting it.

- **Point C (start of the second bar)**: Move your thumb and anchor it on the **A** string, leaning it slightly against the **E** string so you automatically mute both strings. Pick the **D** string with your **index** then **middle finger**. Then do the same on the **G** string, letting both fingers come to rest against the **D** string and muting it.

- **Point D**: As with the earlier exercise, this is the tricky bit—made even trickier because you now have to mute much more quickly due to the eighth notes! Simultaneously move your thumb and anchor it on the **E** string, AND pick the first eighth note on the **A** string with your **index finger** (letting it come to rest on the **E** string), AND lightly mute the **G** string with your **middle finger**. Now immediately play that second quarter note on the **A** string with your **middle finger**—as quickly as you can! Finally pick the **D** string with your **index** then **middle finger**, letting both fingers come to rest against the **A** string and muting it. Phew!

- **Point E (start of the third bar)**: These next two bars are a repeat of the first two, but remember the **D** string you've just played needs to be muted! So treat this the same way as **Point D:** Simultaneously move your thumb and anchor it on the pickup, AND pick the first eighth note on the **E** string with your **index finger**, AND lightly mute the **D** string with your **middle finger**. Now immediately play that second quarter note on the **E** string with your **middle finger**. Finally pick the **A** string with your **index** then **middle finger**, letting both fingers come to rest against the **E** string and muting it.

 ✔ Go back to **Point B** and repeat!

Feel free to experiment with any muting assistance that you can throw into the mix with your fretting hand.

As before, let's take that exercise and move it three frets up the neck!

e Track 39   Example track

 ✔ Stick with the same point-by-point technique from the last exercise, but this time alternate between finger 1 (lower string) and finger 3 (higher string) on your fretting hand.

 ✔ Keep experimenting with using your fretting-hand fingers to assist with the muting—it'll be more of a challenge this time, purely because you're picking the strings twice as fast and giving your fretting-hand fingertips less time to react.

Sticking with the idea of bouncing between the root/tonic and the 5th, let's try it with a reggae style exercise. I've added the extra challenge of basing this 16 bar piece in first position, which makes it *slightly* harder to press the string down.

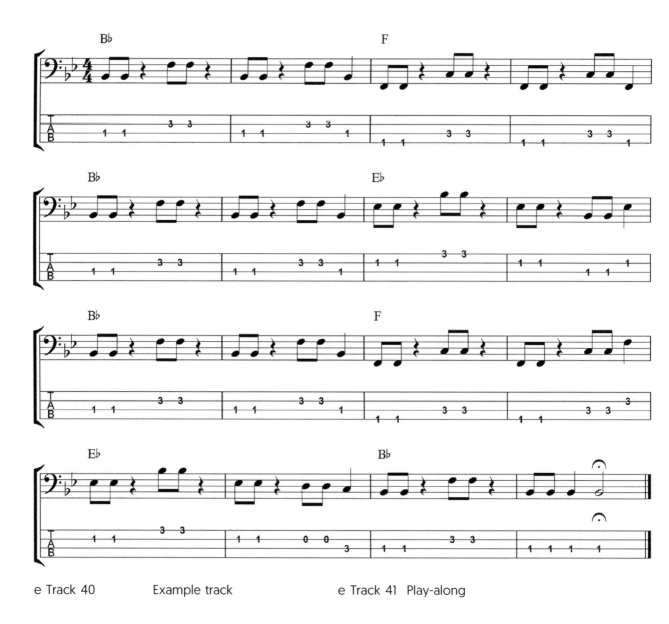

e Track 40   Example track   e Track 41 Play-along

- ✓ The real test in this tune is staying on top of muting when moving between strings. I've thrown a move from an open string into the last line as a small challenge—it'll be harder for the fretting hand to assist with muting.

- ✓ The quarter note rests throughout don't make muting the strings harder—they're just something to be aware of and keep you on your toes! What you definitely want to avoid is letting the notes ring out during those rests.

Still with me? OK, get ready: It's an eighth-note overload with this 12-bar exercise!

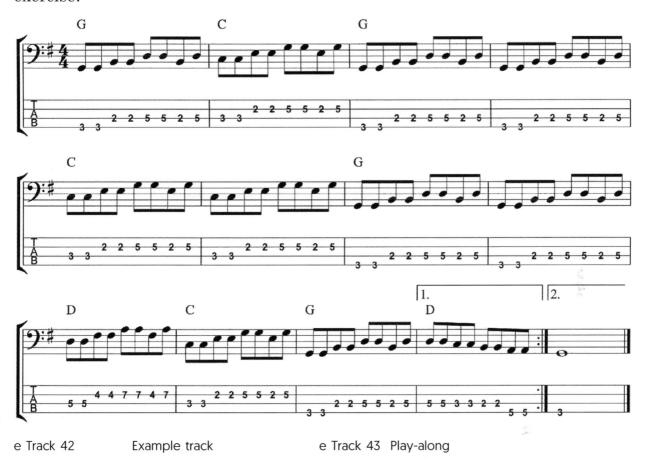

e Track 42   Example track   e Track 43 Play-along

- You can use the fretting hand fingering from the major arpeggios we looked at earlier, including the bars in the last line that play over D major chords. These have the same **Scale Shape** on the fingerboard as the C, F and G arpeggios, meaning they should feel instantly familiar.

- As before, the challenge here is keeping that muting under control when moving between strings, particularly when coming down from a higher to lower string. And you're doing it all with the added pressure of moving at eighth-note speeds! Fortunately this is a challenge that only needs to be performed whilst moving from one bar to the next (apart from the 1° repeat bar where it happens moving between beats 3 and 4) .

✓ The other challenge is a brief shift in position. You can keep your fretting hand in second position for most of this tune, apart from bar 9 (start of the third line of music) where you need to shift up to forth position.

✓ Alternate between your index and middle fingers on your picking hand throughout. And make sure you stop for a break if they start to hurt—picking at this speed can get pretty intense!

After the **5**th, the most common interval that you can find in bass parts is the **Octave.** This would be moving from a low C to a high C (as seen on our "What is a chord" table), or "eight notes up" (hence the "*Oct*" in "*Oct*ave"— think *Octopus, Octagon,* etc.).

Let's dive once again into some fresh technique to get your head around this!

e Track 44   Example track

Octaves — walking up the neck

✓ **Fretting hand fingering:** When playing octaves that don't use open strings, always stick to using finger 1 on the lower string and finger 3 on the higher string. This is pretty much due to human biology—you need the reach between a two-fret/two-string gap that you won't get by using adjacent fingers. Since finger 3 has more strength than finger 4, this is the obvious choice (although feel free to experiment using finger 4 if you prefer!)

- ✅ **Picking + Fretting hand technique:** Each bar here is performed the same way.

  - ✅ **Point A**: Start with your fretting hand thumb anchored on the pickup, and pick the **E** string with your **index finger**. Then simultaneously pick the **D** string with your **middle finger** (letting it come to rest against the **A** string) while using your **index finger** to mute the **E** string.

  - ✅ **Point B**: Slightly trickier! Use the **middle finger** on your picking hand **and/or** the 3rd finger on your fretting hand to mute the **D** string you've just played. At the same time move your picking hand thumb down to rest on the **E** string, AND simultaneously pick the **A** string with your **index finger**. After that, simply pick the **G** string with your fretting hand **middle finger**. And remember you'll need to re-use the muting technique at the start of **Point B** to mute this **G** string before you play the next bar!

I urge you to try this first exercise immediately; you'll see that, amazingly, it's nowhere near as complicated to actually play as it is to explain. What should become very clear at this point is how useful the fretting hand can be for muting (in this case it's actually more-or-less essential). And it's a very easy skill to develop—just keep your finger on the string as you release your hold on the fret, just enough to dampen the vibration.

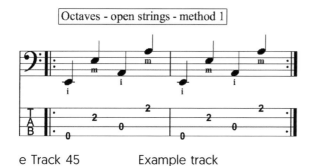

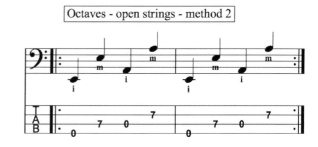

e Track 45   Example track

Octaves — open strings

- ✔ Only one audio track here, since these exercises actually sound the same (check the conventional notation on each — it's identical!) The only difference between them is in the TAB, which illustrates a point I made earlier about it being possible to play exactly the same note in more than one location on the fretboard.

- ✔ **Method 1**: You can apply exactly the same technique from the **Octaves — walking up the neck** exercise to this one, just bear in mind that your picking hand will need to work much harder when it comes to muting. This makes sense if you look at it; there's obviously no need to fret an open string, but it also means there's no fretting hand finger in place to mute that string upon release. Silencing open strings is probably the hardest challenge when it comes to muting, so it's worth spending a bit of time practicing this and finding your own happy muting place!

- ✔ **Method 2**: Weirdly, this is easier to carry off than method 1. Playing the second note in each bar brings your middle finger down from the higher string to rest on the lower string you played before, thereby muting it. Playing the third note in each bar means you just play the same string used for the second note, so muting isn't required. And playing the fourth note mutes the third note in the same way that playing the second note muted the first note! Frankly the only slightly tricky bit is muting the fourth note when

82

you move to the next bar—use the technique from **Point B** in the **walking up the neck** exercise.

We've clearly seen that muting strings while playing octaves is harder to do when you use open strings. So I've been kind and not used any in this octave rock exercise. You're welcome.

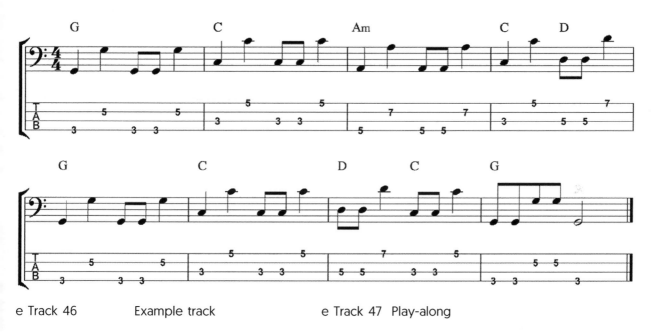

e Track 46   Example track   e Track 47 Play-along

- There's quite a bit of shifting between third and fifth position during this exercise, but you're essentially just moving that distinctive two-string/two-fret gap around the fingerboard. Think of it as a very simple **Scale shape** (guitarists would call this a **Chord shape**) that you can plant anywhere on the neck of the bass.

- I'm truly hoping that your muting is starting to feel instinctive at this point, particularly on your picking hand. Using different anchor points for your thumb as you move up the strings should help silencing any unused lower strings, and it's the tips of your index and middle fingers that are the best tools to use for muting notes when running around octaves.

Now to illustrate a well-established musical equation: **Bass octaves + Fast eighth notes = Disco/Funk**

This has got to be one of *the* quintessential methods for establishing a classic disco feel in a tune. Who needs a drummer anyway?!?

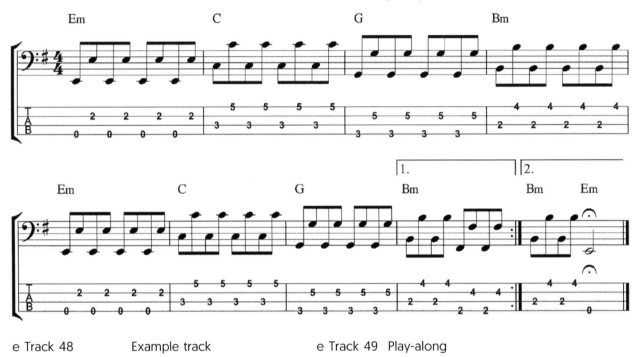

e Track 48   Example track   e Track 49 Play-along

○ Uh-oh, an open **E** string in a full-on octave situation! But don't worry, this one is much easier to deal with from a muting perspective. Firstly, you're playing a repeating pattern, meaning the **index finger** on your picking hand stays hovering right by the string through an entire bar. So you can just rest it back on the **E** string after you've picked it, while your **middle finger** picks the **D** string. Secondly, you're moving up to the **A** string on the next bar, giving you the belt-and-braces opportunity to mute the **E** string with both a shift in thumb position AND bringing the **index finger** that's just picked the **A** back down to rest on the **E**.

○ This is the point where many beginners start to feel that playing eighth notes in octaves is actually easier than playing them on just one string. There's a good reason for this: most people have a longer middle finger than index finger. So if you think about the way your picking hand is positioned in front of the strings, the tip of your middle finger is more ideally placed to play higher strings in relation to your index finger. Given the extraordinary length of many classic disco songs, this is probably a good thing...

I think you've earned a rest here. Let's head back into 3/4 time and wrap up our octave muting with a slow, relaxing waltz.

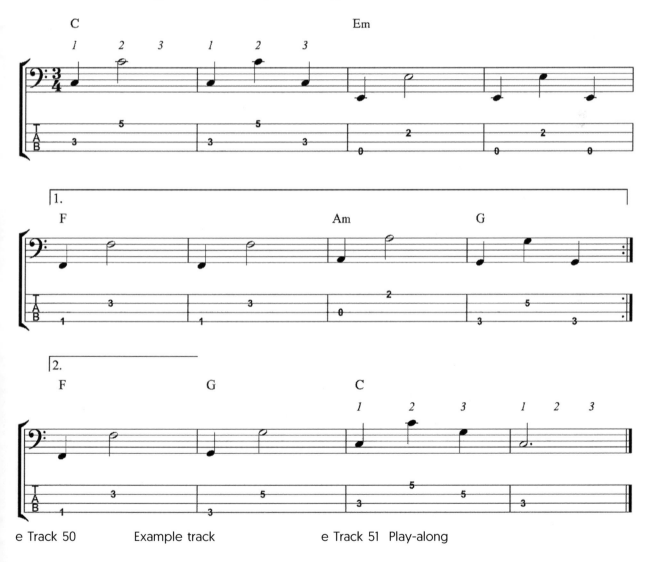

e Track 50   Example track   e Track 51 Play-along

We've got a good mixture of open strings along with octaves played in both first and third positions here. None of this should trouble you, though. Take it nice and slowly, giving the index and middle fingers of your picking hand plenty of time to cover all the string muting required.

You can also see that the 1° and 2° repeats extend over multiple bars for the first time. This works just the same as with individual repeat bars. Play through the first time up to the repeat barline at the end of the 1° section, and go straight back to the start. The second time around you should skip the entire 1° section, jump straight to the 2° section and play to the end of the music.

What's that dot in the last bar all about?!? It's called an **Augmentation dot**, and it tells you to play whatever note it's attached to for 1.5 times the specified duration. Or, to put it another way, a dot adds one half the value of whatever note it's attached to. In this case it's attached to a half note (worth 2 quarter note beats), making that note now last for three quarter note beats in total. This neatly fills an entire 3/4 bar, as you can see from the handy beat numbering included above the stave!

TAKING IT TO THE LIMIT

Expanding your knowledge and technique with rhythm and harmony, all the way up the neck...

CHAPTER XI

Taking Your Rhythm and Harmony Further

A short but important chapter here, introducing two very useful concepts for bass players...

The "Popular Rhythm"

Put very simply, this is when the bass plays on beats 1 and 3, but sort of "anticipates" beat 3 by also hitting the second half of beat 2—a classic example of **Syncopation** which we've already briefly discussed (remember the Latin exercise from earlier?) Some people call this the "classic rhythm," although it doesn't really have an official name. So I'm going to refer to it as the **Popular rhythm,** since it's certainly one of the most common rhythms found in popular music—and the bass guitar is almost always in the driving seat.

Here it is written out for you in a few different styles:

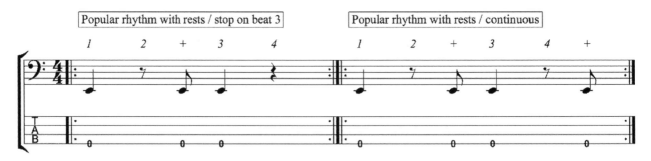

e Track 52   Example track — **Popular Rhythm With Rests**

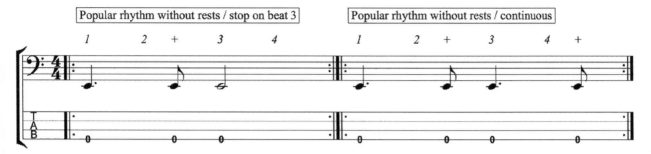

e Track 53   Example track — **Popular Rhythm Without Rests**

● These examples show the Popular rhythm being played in two different ways. The first repeated bar ends the rhythm on beat 3, while the second keeps the bass groove going continuously.

● The example on the top line features rests, breaking the rhythm up and making the bass line feel a little more halting.

● The example on the bottom line fills those gaps in neatly by adding an augmentation dot to the first quarter note beat (extending it by another eighth note duration and covering the rest). This is why you also find rhythms like this referred to as **Dotted rhythms**.

Let's give this popular rhythm two different tries over two different 8-bar exercises.

e Track 54   Example track   e Track 55 Play-along

- A gentle start here (almost a Doobie Brothers feel!) using the popular rhythm with rests and mainly moving in 5ths.

- Don't forget your muting, especially since we're using a lot of open strings here. Those rests need to be just as clearly featured as the notes!

e Track 56   Example track   e Track 57 Play-along

- Remember your C major scale? We're using it here in a gentle lyrical tune, this time with the popular rhythm using dots.

- There's a mixture of movement used on the neck—notes going up and down parts of the scale, with a couple of 5ths and octaves to test your fingering and muting skills as you change between strings.

- No rests here at all, so try and keep this unbroken bass line very smooth!

I can't be discussing all this **Syncopation** and NOT throw another Latin exercise at you! This one is written as a 12-bar blues:

e Track 58   Example track   e Track 59 Play-along

- ● The syncopation is kinda enhanced here, since the second half of beats 2 and 4 in each bar are "anticipating" not just the next beat but ALSO the next note or chord in the music.

- ● No open strings anywhere in this example, so focus your muting skills on making the rests nice and clear. Especially in that 1° repeat bar, where you exclusively play between beats...

- ● This 12-bar has a bit of everything to test your skills — 5ths, octaves, syncopation — but think of it as *"alegría"* (joy) rather than *"loco"* (crazy). And I've numbered the beats in the more complicated bars for you—I'm *bondadoso* like that!

Minor Pentatonic Scales

What are we looking at here?!? Is it a **Scale**?!? Is it an **Arpeggio**?!? Well it's kinda both at once. *And it might be the most useful scale/arpeggio you ever learn.*

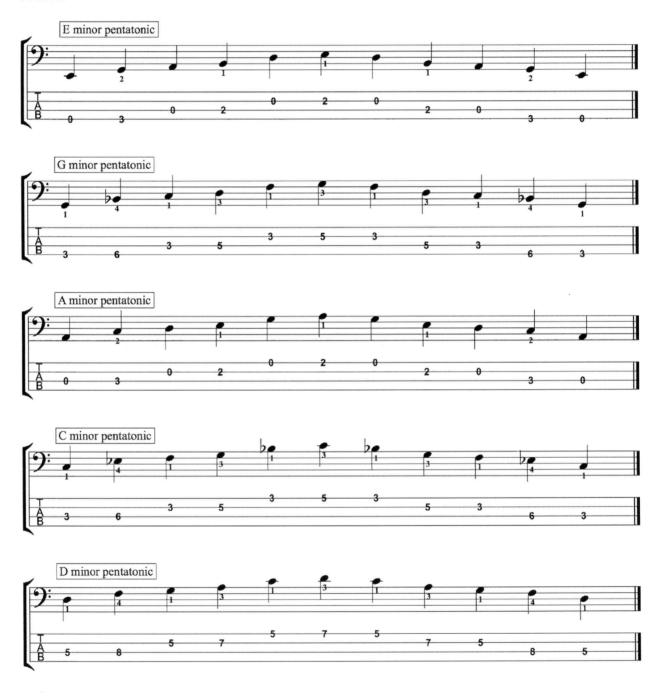

- The **Minor Pentatonic** scale is VERY commonly used throughout music. Particularly blues, and most blues-derived melodies, which is basically most popular music! So a good working knowledge of how to play through it is an invaluable skill for bassists. And THAT is why I've thrown five of them at you in one go...

- Have a play through all of these—no backing tracks needed here, but the fingering has been included to help you. Notice that they all have the same sort of **Scale Shape** as with earlier arpeggios, but the **E** and **A** versions include open strings.

We'll start our Minor Pentatonic exploration with this simple 8-bar Ska/Reggae exercise, moving over the Am and Em versions of the scale.

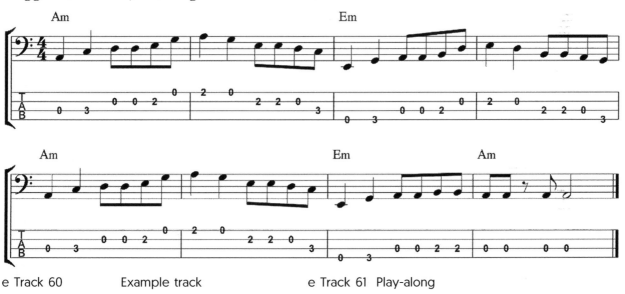

e Track 60   Example track   e Track 61 Play-along

- Nothing more complicated than quarter and eighth notes to worry about for most of this tune, and the first 7 bars use identical rhythms.

- You're working up AND down the full **Am** and **Em** pentatonic scales here, which should hopefully help you start to secure the scale shape.

93

One thing to watch out for is moving between strings—there's plenty of open string use, which makes this just as much of a muting exercise as it is an introduction to the minor pentatonic!

Moving away from open strings now, this gentle jazz ballad uses the **Gm**, **Cm** and **Dm** versions of the scale. And a couple of other new tricks...

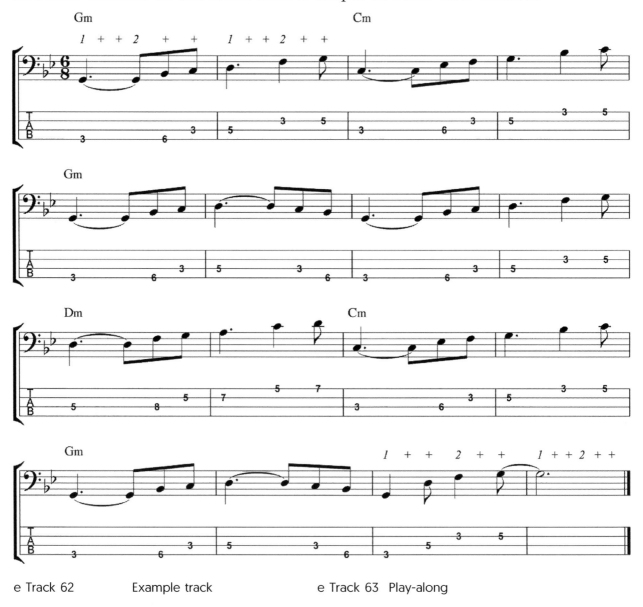

Yes, it's another new **Time Signature** for your collection! 6/8 means that each bar contains six eighth note beats, usually grouped (musically and rhythmically) into two sets of three eighth notes, or "*One-two-three-TWO-two-three*" if you were to count the beat out loud. This is indicated above the stave at the start and end of the example.

● I've also introduced some **Ties** between notes. These literally "tie" the note durations together. If you look at the TAB stave beneath each tie, you'll see that only the first tied note is actually picked; it then carries on ringing through the length of both notes. If you check the end of the exercise you'll see that ties can also cross between bars. Have a listen to the example track to hear this in action.

● Stay in third position for most of this exercise; you only need to move up to the fifth position for the **Dm** section on the third line.

Fifths, **Octaves**, **Syncopation**, **Ties**, **Rests**, **Repeats**—this final 12-bar blues (the last exercise in this book) has got it all!

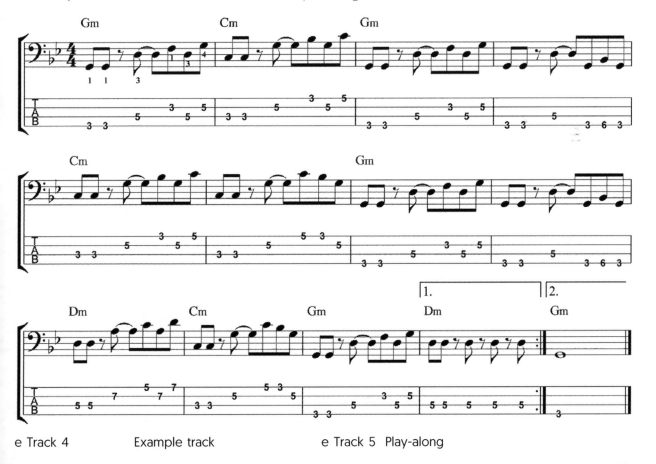

e Track 4   Example track   e Track 5 Play-along

Only part of each minor pentatonic scale is used throughout this bass groove, but feel free to mess around and add a few extra notes here and there. The more comfortable and confident you get with each scale or arpeggio, the more creatively you'll start using them within tunes like this.

Have you noticed we're using the ties as part of the syncopation? Anticipate beat three in each bar, but then hold the note so you don't actually hit beat three. And at this stage I'm confident you can carry this rhythmic stunt off without me needing to label the beats for you!

There is one last, tiny new challenge hidden within this exercise, which will become clear when you try playing through it. Quite a few bars feature adjacent notes on adjacent strings at the same fret (i.e. moving straight from the **A** string at the **5**th **fret** to the **D** string also at the **5**th **fret**). You have a choice here for your fretting hand: either use the fingering I've marked for you in the first bar (so finger 3 on the lower string, finger 4 on the higher string) OR just lay finger 3 across the 5th fret on both strings to create what's known as a **Barre**. That's using your fingers in creative ways!

CHAPTER XII

Moving All Over The Neck

Here's two completely different ways to figure out the position of EVERY SINGLE NOTE on your bass between the headstock and 12ᵗʰ fret.

First let's have a look at them on the bass neck itself with a **Fretboard Diagram**. This is where those **Neck Dots** or **Fret Markers** on the fingerboard start coming in very handy, allowing you to easily and quickly locate the **3ʳᵈ**, **5ᵗʰ**, **7ᵗʰ** and **9ᵗʰ** frets (one dot) along with the **12ᵗʰ** fret (two dots).

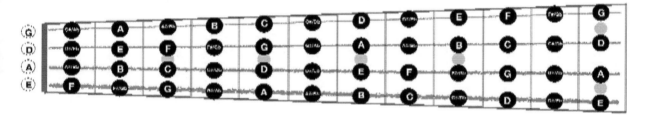

Now let's see them on the conventional and TAB stave, running from the open **E** string all the way up to the **G** string at the 12ᵗʰ fret.

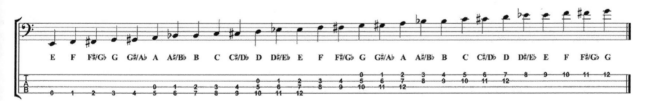

❶ Note that all accidentals are expressed as both a **Flat** (♭) and a **Sharp** (♯). This is because you can describe them in either way, depending on what key you happen to be playing in. It's all down to context due to complicated reasons of music theory, which we fortunately don't need to worry about here!

- Both the bass neck diagram and the TAB show us that some individual pitches can be played in two or three different places on the neck. This demonstrates that benefit of using the TAB stave mentioned back in **Chapter VI,** eliminating the uncertainty of *where you actually play the note*!

It's not completely essential to memorize these diagrams (I'll fully admit that even I can't identify note positions between the 7th and 12th frets without a few moments thought), but a basic knowledge is useful. If you can find a **Root Note** on the neck of your bass, then *you can play any of the scales in this book in that key*!

What we have here are **Scale Diagrams** covering the shape of every scale, arpeggio and pentatonic that you've looked at throughout this book. Remember we covered these in certain keys, or over certain chords, but with these diagrams they're ALL moveable! Just use the fretboard diagram to find out where to base the **Root** (or **Key** or **Tonic**) which is marked as **R.** We've also shown the **3rd**, the **5th** and the Octave (**8ve**) within all scales and arpeggios, giving you many options for finding intervals from root notes.

Major Scale (E string root)

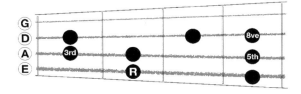

Major Scale (A string root)

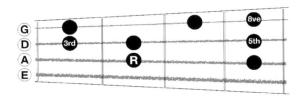

Minor Scale (E string root)

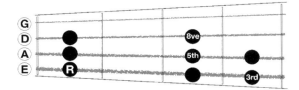

Minor Scale (A string root)

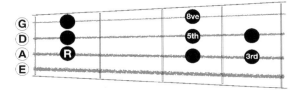

Major Arpeggio (E string root)

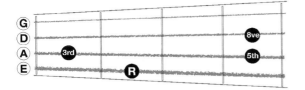

Major Arpeggio (A string root)

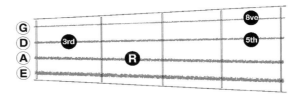

Major Arpeggio (D string root)

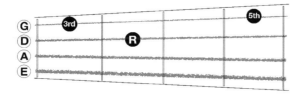

Minor Arpeggio (E string root)

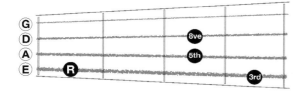

Minor Arpeggio (A string root)

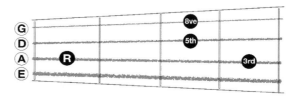

Minor Arpeggio (D string root)

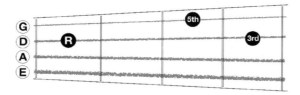

Minor Pentatonic (E string root)

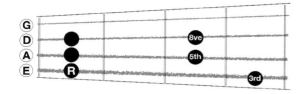

Minor Pentatonic (A string root)

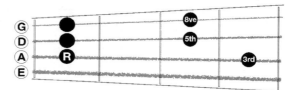

The only other useful scales we haven't looked at use open strings and are based right at the bottom of the neck. Since our moveable **Scale Diagrams** can't cover these, I've written them out individually. Look within the **E** and **A** major and minor scales to find the arpeggios (**R**, **3**rd, **5**th and **8ve** positions) for those keys.

E Major Scale (open E string root)

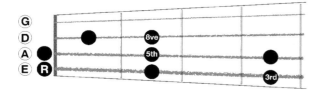

A Major Scale (open A string root)

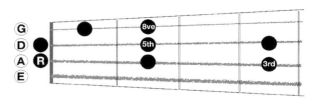

E Minor Scale (open E string root)

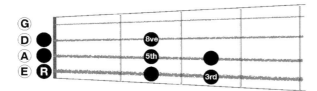

A Minor Scale (open A string root)

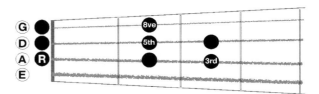

D Major Arpeggio (open D string root)

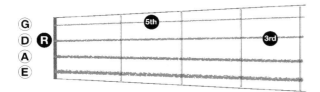

D Minor Arpeggio (open D string root)

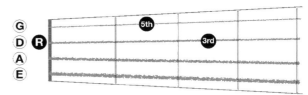

E Minor Pentatonic (open E string root)

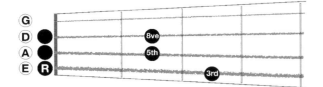

A Minor Pentatonic (open A string root)

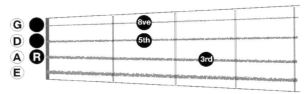

And that's it! The diagrams contained within this chapter should provide all the information you need to play, improvise, jam and genuinely make some wonderful bass noises in ANY key.

You know how to hold your bass.

Your fretting hand knows how to hold down the notes.

our picking hand knows how to pluck the strings.

I think it's safe to say, **"Congratulations — you're a bass player!"**

Well done! I truly hope you've enjoyed the ride. Now go and make some noise...

Postscript: Thoughts on Plectrums

This book has focused on using **Fingerstyle** technique to pick the strings of a bass guitar, mainly to give you maximum control over the instrument. While this is the most common and flexible way of playing, it's also worth knowing how to use a **Plectrum**.

A **Plectrum** (otherwise known as a **Pick**) is simply a flat tool used to pluck the string of a musical instrument. They're usually associated with steel strung guitars, banjos, mandolins, and even harpsichords (yes, there's one plectra for each string inside those things, if you can believe it), but many bass players like to use them as well instead of fingers.

Using a plectrum on the bass guitar produces a different quality of tone from playing fingerstyle—it's slightly more "edgy" and in-your-face. For this reason it's a picking method that's very popular with bassists playing punk, metal and other heavier genres of music.

Many players find they can also pick at higher speeds when using a plectrum compared to fingerstyle. It's also physically easier using a plectrum with your picking hand if you wear your bass slung **really** low on a strap—another important consideration for the rock fans!

- ✓ Plectrums come in a wide range of thicknesses. I'd suggest using a heavier one, since a bass guitar has pretty heavy strings!

- ✓ Plastic is the most common material for plectrum construction (and the type best suited for beginners), but you can also find them made out of wood, bone, and even metal! Queen guitarist Brian May has famously always played his instrument with an old English Sixpence...

- ✓ We should also give a mention to the "First Lady of Bass" on this page. **Carol Kaye** is probably the most prolific session bassist the world has ever known, recording literally tens of thousands of bass parts since the 1950's. Her picking technique of choice (and I'm not joking here) has most commonly been to use a plectrum made of felt!

- ✓ Hold the plectrum firmly between the thumb and index finger of your picking hand, with the end of the pick pointing straight out.

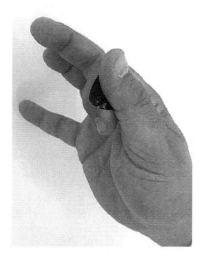

- ✓ Try to keep the rest of your hand and arm relaxed—certainly don't go bunching your hand into a fist!

Using a plectrum will require a different picking hand/arm position to fingerstyle.

- ✓ Try to position the heel of your palm around the top of the strings down towards the bridge.

- ✓ It's sometimes handy to use the pinky of your picking hand as an anchor, just below the strings, so your hand has a useful point of reference.

- ✓ Play the strings using mainly **Downstrokes** for things like half and quarter notes, and a combination of **Downstrokes & Upstrokes** for eighth notes. Try and apply the same force on the strings in either direction so you keep the volume consistent.

Muting when using a pick needs a whole different method to anything we've looked at! This is where keeping the palm of your picking hand near the strings and bridge will come in handy; using it pressed against the strings is the easiest and most obvious method of silencing the strings when you need to.

Your palm also gives the opportunity to try the performance technique known as **Palm Muting**—something that you can't really do when playing fingerstyle. Practice picking the strings while lightly resting your picking-hand palm against them at the point where they leave the bridge. (Don't stray too far or press too hard, otherwise you'll just completely deaden them!) You're aiming to still hear the note, but with a slightly muffled and deadened tone.

Farewell!

Pssssttttt....

What are you doing here? Are you lost?

Do people even look at the last pages of a book?

Jokes aside, I hope you enjoyed this book. I certainly loved the process of writing it.

If you enjoyed this book, could you take 2 minutes to leave a review about it?

Reviews are the lifeblood for small publishers and help us get our books into the hands of more guitarists like you.

We read every review personally and appreciate each one of it.

To leave a review, simply go to the platform you purchased the book from and type in your review.

With that said, here's Guitar Head signing off!

Until next time then? I'll see you in another book.

THE END

Made in the USA
Columbia, SC
12 April 2023

15240467R00059